BUSINESS

DELL

WAY

BUSINESS THE DELL WAY

10 SECRETS of the World's Best Computer Business

REBECCA SAUNDERS

CAPSTONE

Copyright © Rebecca Saunders 2000

The right of Rebecca Saunders to be identified as the author of this work has been asserted in accordance with the Copyright, Designs and Patents Act 1988

First published 2000 by
Capstone Publishing Limited
Oxford Centre for Innovation
Mill Street
Oxford OX2 0JX
United Kingdom
http://www.capstone.co.uk

CIP catalogue records for this book are available from the British Library and the US Library of Congress.
Library of Congress Card Number: 00-105888

ISBN 1-84112-055-3

Typeset in 11/15pt New Baskerville by
Sparks Computer Solutions Ltd, Oxford, UK
http://www.sparks.co.uk
Printed and bound in the UK by
T.J. International Ltd, Padstow, Cornwall

This book is printed on acid-free paper

Substantial discounts on bulk quantities of Capstone books are available to corporations, professional associations and other organizations. For details phone Capstone Publishing on (+44-1865-811113) or fax (+44-1865-240941).

CONTENTS

Dell Computer Corporation may not be the largest computer company, but it does seem to be the fastest growing one. Much of the firm's success is attributed to its direct-sales model. This enables the company to undercut competitive firms on price and to forge closer ties with its customers, while giving shareholders a return several times that of market averages. But direct sales/mass customization of IBM clones is only part of the success story behind Dell Computer Corporation and its founder Michael Dell. In this book we demonstrate that you can have a brilliant business model, but that alone does not create a sustainable advantage. The model often needs to be supported with operational excellence, continuous improvement, and direct input from customers, three of ten leadership secrets of Michael Dell and Dell Computer Corporation that are identified herein.

Michael Dell and Dell Computer Corporation have eliminated the middleman by selling directly to consumers. More importantly, Dell Computer custom-builds IBM clones to the demands of consumers and organizations as communicated via telephone or Internet. Mass customization is regarded by many as the new frontier in business competition. In the computer industry, it certainly is so, as Dell Computer's competitors demonstrate their respect for the technique by taking steps to practice it as well. The competitive advantage it offers is clearly evident. Through mass customization, Dell and his organization can give customers *exactly what they want* generally at a price lower than retail. It's the next best thing to having an uncle in the computer business.

Two: Get Rid of Inventory   **39**
Dell Computer has found that managing the speed of inventory flow can be a winning strategy. Part of that strategy is building strong vendor relationships, ensuring not only parts when needed but quality parts regardless of where manufacture is taking place, since Dell Computer Corporation is truly a global organization. Dell discovered the value of inventory management in 1989 when it bought at prime price more chips than it needed, and then saw prices plummet. Worse, technologically, it found itself with memory chip capacity of 256K to 1 megabyte, thereby being stuck with chips that no one wanted. So Dell has learned the value of inventory management not only from the good times but bad ones as well.

Three: Love Your Suppliers ...   **55**
Dell has learned the value of strategic partnerships with its suppliers to ensure speedy delivery of the latest and best technology. Dell believes in keeping suppliers close geographically, with manufacturing sites near Dell assembly centers around the world, and also keeping suppliers in touch electronically. This heightened communication means better service to Dell and, ultimately, Dell service that will delight customers.

Michael Dell sees himself in a partnership with his employees, one built on bringing the very best to the team. His goal is to hire those not only with the competencies to fill current jobs but also with the potential to fill jobs in the future as the company grows. Dell sees this long-term attitude toward hiring as an additional competitive advantage of Dell, a part of its value chain. It is so responsible for Dell Computer's culture of excellence that Dell takes an active role in meeting with job candidates, including summer interns, to determine if they have the capacity to understand Dell's strategy and if they can help that strategy to evolve. In essence, Dell recruits for succession, and in fact at Dell succession planning is institutionalized, each manager being responsible for finding and developing his or her own successor.

Dell is known for its direct-sales model – and with cause. Dell was the first firm to market PCs by phone. To understand the significance of that step, it's important to realize that at the time Michael Dell went into the computer business the industry as a whole was selling computers through distributors and dealers. The decision gave Dell the ability not only to cut out the middleman but also to reduce inventories, all leading to cost savings that could be passed along to customers. Even more importantly it has enabled Dell to get direct input from customers about their needs and wants. But any discussion of Dell's marketing must include Dell's early decision to take the same model abroad, despite doomsayers who felt the model wouldn't work outside the US. Also, more recently, Dell decided, against opposition from within his own organization, to sell computers on the Internet. Dell currently makes $14 million per day from Internet sales, 30 percent of total revenue, with a longer-term goal of 75 percent.

Dell may be a computer company, but Michael Dell believes
that attention should be on customer needs, not solely technology. That means he and his company focus on the total
customer experience – including service, which Dell sees as
the next competitive frontier. His company's goal is to build
customer loyalty, and he and his management team believe
that the best way to achieve this is by engaging customers in a
dialogue, with the purpose, not of telling them about the advantages of purchasing a Dell product, but of listening to customer likes, needs, and, most important, priorities.

Dell's technological leadership is indicative of the organization's
recognition of the importance of innovation and continuous
improvement, but it also reflects the business's desire to "provide customers with the technology they want." This twofold
objective means that sometimes the organization purchases its
R&D and other times it creates the technology itself. Further,
innovation isn't something limited to the engineering operation. Dell's goal is to hire, in every part of the organization, the
brightest individuals with a willingness to identify operational
shortcomings and seek productive solutions. Dell doesn't want
to run a company in which everyone in the firm thinks the
same way or approaches a situation in the same fashion. He
has said, "By questioning all aspects of our business, we continually inject improvement and innovation into our culture."
This innovative culture is not the only means by which Dell is
catching up with the industry leader, but it is another reason it
is able to attract talented individuals with the desire to make
an impact.

Eight: Think and Act Global 149

Michael Dell took his firm abroad almost a decade before most technology companies. Dell's successful entrance into the UK market in 1987 served as a springboard for operations in Europe, South America and the Asia-Pacific region, including most recently China. In each global expansion, the decision met with criticism and doubt. In particular, Dell's movement into the Pacific was met with naysayers who felt that the direct-sell model was a Western concept and wouldn't work in the Pacific Rim. But sales figures have shown otherwise. Dell has found that sticking to the direct-sell model is the most effective way to go global, at the same time adapting to local practice. For example, in Germany fax numbers are provided for initial customer enquiries, Germans preferring not to telephone in response to an ad.

Nine: Stay True to Your Talents 167

There is a saying, "Don't mess with success." This doesn't mean that Michael Dell believes, as another saying goes, "If it ain't broke, don't fix it." He clearly has fine-tuned his direct-sales/ mass-customize model over the years. But experience has taught him the value of staying true to your talents. For Dell Computer Corporation these are: (1) disdain inventory; (2) listen to your customers; and (3) sell direct. Many excellent companies encounter troubles when they forget those qualities that made them excellent, and move instead in directions where they lack strengths – not so Dell.

Ten: Manage Hypergrowth 181

Dell learned the hard way that the secret to successful business expansion is *managed growth*. In the second quarter of 1993, Dell Computer experienced several expansion problems, including failure of a line of low-quality laptops. There is clearly the danger of an upstart "getting too far ahead of itself," expanding so fast that it finds it cannot meet commitments to customers, employees, and shareholders. As Dell has said, from its startup an organization has to figure out where it will focus as it takes on one challenge after another, making its selection from among those opportunities that are not only the best but also represent most effective and efficient use of its strengths.

◆ PREFACE ◆

Michael Dell recently wrote a book that recounts his founding of Dell Computer Corporation. The book entitled *Direct from Dell*, written with Catherine Fredman, describes step by step the founding of what is currently the second-largest computer producer. In his book, Dell describes many of the steps that led to the business' formation and also discusses the management actions that were subsequently taken to grow the business. This book, too, describes the founding of Dell Computer Corporation and subsequent actions taken by Michael Dell. But unlike the Dell book, which does this and nothing else, this book looks at the reasons for the actions taken and puts them in the greater management context.

In the Introduction to this book, I describe Michael Dell as a "methodical optimizer," someone who found a business model that worked and who has subsequently consistently applied that model with obvious success. But there is much more to the success of Dell Computer Corporation. This book identifies ten leadership strengths that Michael Dell exhibits and, more important, positions these strengths in terms of the leadership competencies that organizations of today demand.

As in my earlier book about Jeff Bezos, which was based on numerous articles by fellow business journalists, this book, too is based on articles about and interviews with Michael Dell by business reporters, as well as his own book. But the contents also reflect 25-plus years of my own in business/management reporting and writing, during which I have met numerous entrepreneurs and corporate presidents as well as the many gurus who often tell them how to manage. Consequently, my reflections on Dell are well grounded by my own knowledge of best practices and latest management thinking.

Why should you purchase this book? What will you find in it for yourself? Besides insights into this quiet man who is dramatically changing the way business in the computer industry is done, you should find strategies to help grow your own business, including issues and caveats that you need to consider as you go about your own business of making a success of your firm. On the cover jacket of Michael Dell's book *Direct from Dell,* the book's publishers describe the book as "both an extraordinary business success story and a manifesto for revolutionizing any industry." If I were writing the jacket for this book, I would describe it as a "leader's guide" not only to help you better appreciate the Dell success story but also write your own story of corporate success. It doesn't matter if you are an entrepreneur of an upstart firm, a division VP of an established firm, or the senior officer of a major corporation, there are lessons here about management that you can put to use. And that's what a management book should give you: practical help and insights.

Rebecca Saunders

SUCCEEDING, THE MICHAEL DELL WAY

"The closest person we have to Henry Ford
is Michael Dell."
– Fortune

The "nerds" may be winners, as Tom Peters has declared, but they are winners, not because of their lifelong love affair with technology, but because of their entrepreneurial instincts – in particular, their ability to hold to a clear, compelling strategy. We have all heard about Bill Gates and we are increasingly learning about the management strategies of Webmaster Jeff Bezos, CEO and founder of Amazon.com. Another entrepreneur who has clearly defined the nature of the business and then tailored a system to ensure its successful implementation is Michael Dell, chairman and chief executive officer of Dell Computer Corporation. The organization that Dell heads is innovative, always searching for ways to improve the value of its products and to exceed customer expectations, and of course adapt to the changing external environment. Yet, in the process, it has learned the value of staying with a single strategy: to sell direct to customers. By building computers tailored to customers' desires often at below-retail prices, Dell has differentiated itself from other PC firms.

When Dell has strayed from this single focus, his business has suffered. In 1991, for instance, Dell Computer decided to expand beyond telemarketing to retail, selling through computer superstores and warehouse clubs. The numbers quickly prompted Dell to withdraw from retail.

DELL'S SORT OF ENTREPRENEUR

Success noted that there are two kinds of entrepreneurs: "the deal junkies" who rush from one new venture or market to another, sometimes finding a pot of gold but more often not; and "the methodical optimizers," entrepreneurs who found a company based on a good idea and then build on that idea, constantly improving on it and, yes, adapting when the opportunities exist but never losing that strategic focus. Dell is the latter.

Dell's direct business model is behind the firm's continued success. Competitively, it:

◆ eliminates the need to support an extensive network of wholesale and retail dealers, in turn eliminating dealer markups;

◆ avoids higher inventory costs associated with "best estimates" of product demand;

◆ avoids large inventories of obsolescent finished products due to the rapidly changing technological market; and

◆ gives the firm the ability to maintain, monitor, and update a customer database that can be used to shape future product offerings and post-sales service and support programs.

The bottom line – and of course that's where the direct business model must truly be weighed – is that Dell Computer Corporation is able to bring the latest technology to its customers faster and more competitively priced than many of its competitors.

Most recently Dell has taken the idea of directly selling to customers on the Web, and sales at Dell's Web site now make up 30 percent of corporate business.

THE REAL BEGINNINGS

Most writers point to the start of Dell's business career in 1984 while he was an undergraduate at college, but signs were already evident when at the age of twelve, with a reseller's license, he conducted a nationwide mail-order stamp auction, making for himself a profit of $2000. Always interested in founding his own business, he sold subscriptions for a Houston newspaper. Dell told reporters that he realized that the majority of new subscribers were either new to Houston or recently married, so he researched public records of new home purchases and marriage license applications at the county clerk's office to find prospects. "I sold a lot of newspapers," he recalls. He had started his newspaper-subscription business during the summer, and it proved so lucrative that he continued it once he returned to high school, doing the work during the week after school and on Saturday mornings.

> He was making about $18,000 a year, more money annually than his then high-school teacher

He was making about $18,000 a year, more money annually than his then high-school teacher of history and economics. She discovered this when she assigned her class to file their tax return. At first, she thought he had misplaced the decimal place. "When she realized I hadn't, she was dismayed," Dell recalls.

His fascination "with the idea of a machine that could compute things" began, he says, even before high school – when he was seven years old and purchased his first calculator. By the time he was in high school, computers had become a hobby. He would hang around the nearby Radio Shack and play with the computers, saving his money to buy his own. His first purchase was an Apple computer, which he immediately disassembled when he got it home. "I wanted to see how it worked," he explains.

When IBM came out with its PC, Dell switched his allegiance to it, seeing its business applications more marketable over the long term than Apple whose selling point at the time was games. Dell would purchase a PC, upgrade it with more memory, bigger monitors, faster modems, or whatever, and then sell it. Most guys his age would be souping up their car but Dell, whose room by then looked like a mechanic's shop, was going to distributors to purchase components in bulk to increase his profit margin on computers he sold.

As Dell familiarized himself with the computer industry, he discovered the huge markups on retail sales. At the time, IBM PCs were bought by dealers for $2000 and sold to consumers for $3000, making $1000 in profits, without service support. Dell was already making money from selling computers, but he realized that he could actually compete with computer stores on both price and service, by communicating about PCs with other people via a bulletin board system on the early Web. But Dell's parents had another plan for their son: college.

Off he went to the University of Texas in Austin. But he had not forgotten that there was "a lot of opportunity" in the computer business. He drove off in the white BMW he had bought from his subscription business profits *with three computers in the backseat of the car.*

In college, he got even more into the computer business. A pre-med student, he attended classes, then went back to his dorm room where he would upgrade a few computers. Word got out, and soon he had customers – attorneys and doctors and instructors, not only students – lining up to have him service their computers. He had applied for a vendor's license and received one, and from his dorm room was able to sell high-performance computer models at much less cost than a computer store with overheads to consider. He won lots of bids. He was able to undersell far larger, more established competitors, because he had eliminated the middleman, who added little to the process except a substantial markup.

His avocation, soon career, began to affect his grades. When his parents showed up on a surprise visit to find out what was happening, he had barely enough time to stash the various parts in a friend's dorm room. Despite his plea, "I want to compete with IBM PC," Dell's parents demanded he give up the computer business, he recalls. He tried, but in a short time he recognized that his interest in computers wasn't a phase.

On January 2, 1984, he formed and registered his company PC's Limited. Over the next five months, he moved out of the dorm into a condominium from which he sold upgraded PCs, upgrade kits, and add-on components. In early May, he incorporated the firm as Dell Computer Corporation doing business as PC's Limited. He was making more than $50,000 a month at that time. His grades were another thing, however. He finished his freshman year and left.

At first Dell only purchased stripped-down computers, added disk drives and memory, upgraded them, and then sold them for a profit. But he quickly realized that the real money could be made in making his own PCs. With the development of chip sets by Gordon Campbell, he recalls, it was much easier to design PCs. Dell got the name of a local engineer, Jay Bell, and asked him if he could design one. Bell asked for $2000, and in a week and a half he had earned his $2000. Dell had its first 286-based PC.

THE SECOND LARGEST PC PRODUCER

Since then, Dell Computer Corporation has become the second largest PC manufacturer in the US, with nearly 21,000 employees. As Dell shows signs of gaining on the leader of the pack, that leader, Compaq, has been prompted to emulate Dell, entering into the custom computer business itself.

When the idea to sell computers directly to users was first proposed by Dell, it didn't meet with the approval that has come from eleven years of success.

However, when the idea to sell computers directly to users was first proposed by Dell, it didn't meet with the approval that has come from eleven years of success. "Michael had many people who were very good, very professional, that would have been willing to state on a stack of bibles 'you can't do it.' And he did it," according to David Huss, a writer about software who used to sell computer parts to Dell shortly after he quit college.

What makes Dell's sales model so worthy of imitation? Because computers are built based on real orders from end-users, there is no need to depend on forecast market demands in what is a highly volatile computer market, and there are no unnecessary parts or aged computers sitting on warehouse shelves. Which means that the company is able to keep manufacturing costs way down. Orders today come not only from phone but via Dell's Web site, www.dell.com, where it maintains 44 company-specific sites. There are around two million visitors per week, and the firm does around $14 million in sales every day. By the end of the fourth quarter of fiscal year 1999, sales accounted for 25 percent of revenue for that quarter. A worldwide company, the organization has manufacturing facilities in the Americas and Europe, and now in China and Brazil. The assembly process takes about five hours – including testing prior to shipment. Says Campbell Matter, a Dell investor, the computer user gets "that perfect BTO, built-to-order model, where everybody can configure what they want. He gives you the Rolls Royce quality, the Mazerati speed, and he gives you that Volkswagen Beetle price."

Sales as of mid-1999 were at $5.5 billion. The company most recently reported a 42 percent rise in profit during the first quarter, to $434 million. By next year, the company expects to see direct sales of personal computers over the Internet to contribute up to 50 percent of total revenue. Once that is reached, according to Dell's vice-chairman Kevin Rollins, the company will set a new goal of probably 75 percent of business via the Internet.

Dell is the first to admit that his decision to sell directly to customers was prompted by necessity and not any great insights into the way business would move in the future. "At the root of it," he has told the press, "I was opportunistic." On the other hand, Dell knew that he had a good thing when he found it and he hasn't swayed from "mass customization," which many industrial gurus regard as the paradigm for the next century. But concept isn't enough; businesses survive and thrive on execution and it is this that has earned Dell so many honors, like "Entrepreneur of the Year" from *Inc.* magazine (1989), "Man of the Year" from *PC Magazine,* and "CEO of the Year" for 1993 by *Financial World* magazine.

PC Laptop magazine named Dell "Portable Pioneer" in 1994. Two years later, he was honored with the title "Best CEO of a Turnaround" by *Upside Magazine* because of Dell's resurgence in the notebook market and success in the global markets. In 1997, he was included in *Business Week*'s list of "The Top 25 Managers of the Year."

Wall Street marked Dell's executive leadership with the *Wall Street Transcript's* Gold Award in 1991; the year before he got the Silver Award.

What is behind all these managerial honors? Dell's success can be attributed to ten leadership secrets:

1   Build to order. Dell eliminates the middleman by custom-building IBM clones and selling them directly to consumers, thereby reducing overhead costs and eliminating dealer markups. This is the original marketing concept behind Dell Computer.

2   Value and manage inventory. This is a direct consequence of Dell's sell-and-build approach to the manufacture of PCs.

3   Ally with suppliers. Highest quality comes from out-
    sourcing manufacture of parts to suppliers with most ex-
    pertise, experience, and quality in producing that part.

4   Ally with employees. Hire those who can generate ideas,
    train people to be creative, and create an environment
    that allows ideas to be tested.

5   Market innovate. Dell was the first firm to market PCs by
    phone but $14 million in sales daily today comes from
    business on the Web. As Michael Dell says, be alert to op-
    portunities outside traditional distribution channels.

6   Focus on the total customer experience. Neither focus on
    computers nor competitors nor customers alone. Consider
    the entire customer process, and ensure a positive experi-
    ence throughout.

7   Innovate or disappear. On the other hand, recognize that
    gradual improvements to each product line reduce risk
    and allow you to take advantage of rapid technological
    developments.

8   Think and act global. A young Dell Computer – and young
    Michael Dell – established the first of 12 international op-
    erations. He took his firm abroad almost a decade before
    most technology companies.

9   Don't mess with success. Stay the course. If the formula
    works, don't mess with it. Dell has learned that it is best to
    come up with a good idea, stay with it to be sure it is a
    good idea, then tirelessly pursue that idea.

THE BUSINESS TIMES OF MICHAEL DELL

◆ **1980** Michael Dell buys his first computer – an Apple II – and dismantles it to see how it works.

◆ **1983** Michael Dell heads for the University of Texas, promising his parents to put aside his interest in computers to study biology. But in the back of his car he carries three computers ready for upgrading and sale.

◆ **1984–88** Michael Dell begins his computer business at the University of Texas, reportedly often hiding his IBM PCs in his roommate's bathtub when family members visit; Dell leaves.

◆ **1984** Dell registers the company with the State of Texas as "PC's Limited." Five months later, he incorporates the company as "Dell Computer Corporation, doing business as PC's Limited."

◆ **1987** Dell opens an office in the UK. Over the next ten years, Dell opens offices in 33 countries.

◆ **1988** Dell takes the company public with sales at $59 million and 650 employees; Dell averages 300,000 orders each day in the US alone.

◆ **1991** Dell introduces its first notebook PC.

◆ **1992** Dell becomes one of the top five PC makers worldwide.

◆ **1993** Dell moves into the Asia-Pacific region with subsidiaries in Australia and Japan.

◆ **1995** Dell begins construction of the Asia Pacific Customer Center in Penang, Malaysia. Dell now has manufacturing sites in the US, Ireland, Malaysia, China and Brazil.

◆ **1996** Dell goes on the Web, opening its Web site www.dell.com. Sales today are estimated at $14 million daily.

◆ **1996** Dell makes major push into the network-server market.

◆ **1997** Dell unveils its first workstation systems.

- **1998** Dell expands manufacturing facilities in the Americas and Europe and opens production and customer center in Xiamen, China.
- **1999** Dell once again proves the skeptics wrong when he takes his direct model to Brazil.
- **1999** Dell publishes his book *Direct from Dell*, written with Catherine Fredman.
- **1999** Dell founds Dell Ventures, an investment arm that within a year had put $70 million into 88 companies. Dell Ventures will not only invest in companies but also provide assistance with strategy development and providing access to professional services.
- **1999** Dell launches a group called Gigabuys to resell software, printers, digital cameras and, more recently, office equipment.
- **2000** Dell buys a stake in StorageNetworks and will resell that company's Web-storage service. Other partners: fast Search & Transfer and CenterBeam.
- **2000** Dell founds www.DellEworks.com, a new small business site that provides customers a one-stop source to establish an Internet presence and grow businesses with online services.
- **2000** Dell and Microsoft partner with Government Technology magazine to create a Web portal (egov.govtech.net) where visitors can learn about advances and best practices in digital government.

10 Manage growth, even hypergrowth. When you grow, don't grow for growth's sake. Dell learned this the hard way. In the second quarter of 1993, Dell Computer experienced several expansion problems, including failure of a line of low-quality laptops. Growth is good, but it's controlled growth.

BIBLIOGRAPHY

Dell, Michael and Fredman, Catherine, *Direct from Dell: Strategies That Revolutionized an Industry*, HarperBusiness, New York 1999.

Goldstein, Mark L., "An Industry Legend – at 21: Mike Dell is the Latest Wunderkind of the Computer Industry," *Inc.*, April 20, 1987.

Murphy, Richard, "Michael Dell," *Success*, January 1999.

One

MASS CUSTOMIZE!

To all our nit-picky – over-demanding – ask-awk-ward-questions customers: Thank you, and keep up the good work.
– Dell Advertisement

Build-to-order would seem to be one of the hottest manufacturing trends going and, according to management gurus, it will have as much impact on manufacturing as did the advent of mass production and mass marketing in the nineteenth century. It supports a customer-focused approach to operating a business, at the same time enabling that company to practice just-in-time inventory management, and thereby reap the cost benefits of manufacturing agility. Mass customization is the answer to the ever-increasing demand of today's customers not only for high-quality and low-costing products but variety and *even* uniqueness in what they purchase.

Erick Schonfeld, writing in *Fortune* magazine, terms the mass customization movement "a silent revolution."

UNDERSTAND THE BENEFITS OF MASS CUSTOMIZATION

Michael Dell is well aware of the benefits of direct sell. "Be Direct" was the sales model for Dell Computer Corporation from its founding in Dell's dorm. The model called for the firm to serve customers directly over toll-free phone lines. Only after a computer was sold were the parts ordered, thereby eliminating the cost of dealer fees and maintenance of a large inventory. Savings were passed on to customers. Dell told a reporter, "There is a great advantage in the direct model because of how the sales cycle works. In the indirect model, there are two sales forces: there is the one from the manufacturer to the dealer and then another from the dealership's sales to the customer. In the direct model we have just one sales force and it is totally focused on the customer – our customer."

In today's times, when customers call the shots, this model is especially appropriate. From the startup of Dell Computer, the entire company – from research and development to manufacture to sales – has been listening to the customer, responding to the customer, and delivering what the customer asked for, in line with the direct model.

Interestingly, the same three strengths that the company identified in its youth remain – and all are linked to the sales concept of "Dell Direct":

◆ *High-performance products.* The standard, then, was set by IBM, and that was what customers wanted – and what Dell offered.

◆ *Direct relationship with customers.* Dell had an ongoing dialogue with customers. The information gave the company a competitive advantage in tailoring its products and communications to customer thinking. Direct marketing also avoided dealer markups. This remains true today – even with the prices of PCs declining, such rates may still be as high as a quarter of purchase price.

◆ *Efficient and flexible manufacturing.* The fledgling firm didn't have much capital and the issue of inventory was a serious one. Although the firm now garners most of the market share, it continues to monitor inventory levels, practicing JIT to remain flexible to build machines to customers' orders.

SUCCESS STRATEGIES IN A DOT-COM ECONOMY

Dr George Weathersby, president and CEO of the American Management Association, has identified six factors critical to organizations in today's dot-com economy. Writing his "Weathersby Report" at AMA's *MWorld* (www.amanet.org), the membership site for the global training and publishing organization, Weathersby cites six factors for success, suggesting that businesses need to transform themselves to incorporate these six:

◆ innovation;
◆ build to order, mass customization;
◆ customer-driven fulfillment;
◆ proactive, personalized services;
◆ total reliability and quality; and
◆ lifetime relationship.

Weathersby writes that successful organizations will be those that excel at one-to-one marketing, tailoring their contact strategy and messaging to the interest of each customer. He notes the impact of customer input in achieving each, even innovation. "Innovation is the result of customer action, not of corporate action." It is a customer's needs or wants that lead to conception of a product, not marketing or the R&D department's creativity. Once the product is conceptualized, he suggests, the company builds the product and then delivers it in the manner also chosen by the customer.

This six-step process makes the difference between being the "Deller" – the winning firm – or the "Dellee" – the market loser.

Although "Be Direct" has undergone some adaptation since those early days, it continues to be the operating principle for Dell. In 1991, as the company experienced a major growth spurt, it violated one of what Dell calls its "three golden Dell rules": *never sell indirect*. (The other two are: *disdain inventory* and *always listen to the customer*.) The company chose to join its competitors and sell its products through dealers. But, four years later, it learned that while it was successfully selling PCs via the retail channels, it wasn't making any money. Nor were its competitors! Consequently, Dell withdrew from the retail business. Dell recalled: "Every news story on the subject said that Dell was severely limiting its growth by going out of retail." But as history proved, it was not a mistake.

> **"Every news story on the subject said that Dell was severely limiting its growth by going out of retail."**
> **– Michael Dell**

Not only was retail only a small part of Dell's business at the time, but as Dell has told business leaders, the move out of retail forced all corporate attention back on direct sales where the company was truly successful. Attention went to the cost benefits of also using the direct model to reduce inventory well below the levels of competitors. There were skeptics – both within and outside the company – but the company was able in four years to increase sales sixfold (from $2.9 billion to $12.3 billion) while raising annual inventory costs by only $13 million (from $220 million in 1993 to $233 million). Currently inventory is down to eight and frequently as few as seven days. Boasts Dell, "We're starting to measure it in hours."

Purchasing online may be a little more complex than speaking to a sales rep by phone, but Dell.com has been created to make shopping and buying on the Web relatively easy. You select a system of interest, customize and price it, then get a final quote on your system, place your order online or save it for later submission or e-mail another to get a second opinion, retrieve a saved order, or upgrade your current system. If you have questions, there is an 800 number to call for sales help. Within 90 days of Dell selling on the Internet, it was making $2 million a week. Customers found ordering over the net saved them time, allowed them to access in-depth information in real time, and later have a wealth of service information available to them. The company also found that only half as many phone calls per customer were needed to make a sale and the average system selling price was higher over the net. Further, Dell.com contained informational updates that were building customer brand loyalty.

Of course, Dell's success with build-to-order has not gone unnoticed by its competitors such as Compaq, which in November 1998 made a major push to sell built-to-order computers directly to customers over the Internet. And understandably so. Dell's direct-sell model (which uses the Internet, phone orders, and an outsourced sales force) has allowed the Round Rock, Texas-based firm to overtake Compaq as the No. 1 seller to US business, with 19 percent of the market, and fueled annual earnings growth of 70 percent from 1996 to 1999. Said William Schaub, vice-president of personal computing for Dataquest, a research and consulting firm in San Jose California, "Compaq had to move to build-to-order to stay competitive. Once an order is placed, Dell can build a box in six hours. That's not the way it has been done at Compaq."

FOUR WAYS TO CUSTOMIZE

If you are interested in exploring whether mass customization would work for your firm, it may help you to know about four basic approaches, according to James B. Gilmore and B. Joseph Pine II writing in *Harvard Business Review*.

♦ *Collaborative.* Firms that practice this approach conduct dialogues with customers to help them articulate their needs, identify the precise offerings that meet these needs, and make customized products for them. It's best used for businesses whose customers can't easily articulate what they want and become frustrated when forced to select from multiple choices – firms like Paris Miki, a Japanese eyewear retailer that offers myriad eyeglass designs. The firm's Mikissimes Design System uses a digital picture of each consumer's face as well as a statement from the customer about the look he or she wants to recommend a distinctive lens size and shape, then displays the lenses on the digital image of the consumer's face.

♦ *Adaptive.* These firms offer one standard product but it is customizable. The adaptive approach is best for firms whose customers want products to perform in different ways on different occasions. Consider Lutron Electronics Company of Coopersburg, PA, whose customers want its systems to maximize productivity at the office or create appropriate moods at home without being forced to experiment with multiple switches each time they want a new effect. The Grafik Eye System, therefore, connects different lights in a room and allows the user to program different effects for lively parties or quiet evenings at home. The lights come with programmed settings to make it all very easy for the customer.

♦ *Cosmetic.* These firms offer a standard product but they offer it differently to different customers. It isn't the product that is customized or customizable but the offering. Maybe it's the display, or it's the way the product's attributes are advertised. The product may not be truly personalized but the merchandising is still of value to the potential customer. So the Planters Company, a Nabisco division, now packages its peanuts and mixed nuts in various containers and sizes to merchants with different customer demands.

◆ *Transparent.* Companies provide individual customers with unique goods or services without letting them know explicitly that those products or services have been customized for them. This approach works, of course, when customers' specific needs are predictable or easily deduced, but customers do not want to be asked their choices repeatedly. Transparent customizers monitor customers' behavior without direct interaction and then quietly customize their offerings within a standardized package. A case in point: ChemStation of Dayton, Ohio, that produces an industrial soap for use in car washes and factory floors. Purchasers may not care that the company spent considerable time learning about customers' usage patterns; they just care that it works for their specific application.

BE REALISTIC ABOUT THE WORK INVOLVED

Since Dell's success, IBM and other competitors have adapted custom manufacturing methods, but so far they have failed to match Dell. Dell competitors' computers have sold primarily through resellers and by moving to direct sales these firms risk alienating dealerships, which they need to sell to big businesses and consumers. (Dell's consumer sales are a very small piece of its business.) Besides, direct-selling may seem simple but it is far from so. Keith Maxwell, vice-president for Dell world operations, pointed out how a tour of Dell's showroom plant, Metric 12, in Round Rock might leave one with the impression that it is easy, but it is far from so. "If you walk into Metric 12," he told a reporter "everything looks so smooth. But what it takes underneath to make all that material and those orders and those product releases all happen on time is a lot of very smart and dedicated people."

The factory Maxwell designed runs on 54 powerful server computers (Dell, of course), tracking orders, inventory and work status, downloading precisely the right software to each computer. Bar-code readers record computer progress through the factory. Then servers automatically download the exact software that each customer has ordered. In all, workers touch the computers around eighteen times – the fewer times, the less chance of damage. All products that leave the plant are tested; first, they undergo a brief test to identify any assembly problems, then they go to have software downloaded, after which they undergo further tests to ensure all is well before a worker places a large suction tube on the finished computer to lift it from the assembly line and place it in a shipping box.

As Dell business has moved increasingly away from individual consumers to corporate and institutional accounts, so, too, Dell has adjusted its tracking, planning, and scheduling software to monitor the progress of an account's entire order rather than individual computers being assembled.

Production is a collaborative effort, demanding considerable coordination among sales, production, and product engineering. According to Maxwell, most companies become compartmentalized. Dell insists that its teams work together – and it should be obvious why. If there is no communication between sales and manufacturing, efficiency can be destroyed. Maxwell observed, "Metric 12 requires that the whole organization be integrated." There isn't any fat in either schedules or inventory to cope with last-minute problems. "There is no way to let things pile up because you have no piles."

MASS PRODUCTION VS. MASS CUSTOMIZATION

Yes, mass production is cost-efficient but mass customization can be even more efficient, allowing organizations to significantly slash inventory costs. And, most important, it enables a company to better service customers. No question, the time is right for mass customization, too. The technology is available – like computer-controlled assembly lines that can quickly be adjusted, bar-code scanners that track both parts and finished products, databases that contain bytes of information about each customer's wants, digital printers that change product packaging with a few keystrokes, and logistics and supply-chain management software to coordinate manufacturing and distribution. There is even a means by which mass-customized products can be sold one-by-one: the Internet. In his book *Mass Customization: The New Frontier in Business Competition,* B. Joseph Pine, II, co-founder of Strategic Horizons LLP, points out how the Web makes it possible for companies to conduct an ongoing, one-on-one dialogue with each of their customers to determine exactly their wants and needs. But, perhaps more important, the Internet enables customers to learn which enterprise has the best offering. Every day, as we come to work, the impact of the Internet is evident. But it is even greater in the marketplace, where information about another company's products is only a mouse click away for not only us but our customers.

Regis McKenna considers customization one indicator of the increased power of customers today, as he observes in his book *Relationship Management: Successful Strategies for the Age of the Customer.* Price can't sustain customer loyalty – nor can innovation – it's too easy to duplicate another firm's creativity. Brand loyalty is no more valuable today, either. As McKenna observes, "Choice has become a higher value than brand in America."

UNDERSTAND THE ROLE OF CUSTOMIZATION IN THE BUSINESS EQUATION

Of course, manufacturers aren't the only firms that can offer customization. For instance, hotel chains offer a number of options: non-smoking versus smoking rooms, corner versus side rooms, king-sized versus double beds, different floors, closeness to fire exits and amenities such as pools and exercise equipment, concierge services, and so forth. Through a "guest recognition" system, Marriott goes a step further, storing information about guest preferences in a central database that can be accessed locally so Marriott hotels can provide business road warriors with the rooms, services, and amenities of their choice.

Hertz, too, has its own database as part of its #1 Club Gold program, recording the types of automobiles customers prefer and trucking in these cars to have the right mix of vehicles on hand. A Gold customer pays an annual premium for the service, but it means he or she can go directly to the special Gold area, place luggage in the trunk of his or her car in a weather-protected stall, and check in at the exit gate. At many locations, when the customer returns, there is a Hertz representative who will come to the car to handle the return via a hand-held computer rather than require the customer to stand in line at the checkout counter.

In service industries, the key is customizing services around standardized offerings. In the case of manufacturers, customization is more complex, requiring changes in the product or process by which differentiated products are produced. In most instances, differentiation of a product occurs at the last possible step in the supply chain. But the product is designed so it can be easily assembled, relying on modules that have use in a number of products. The manufacturing process is broken into steps or modules that can be moved or rearranged to support various designs.

> ... computers have been made to customer specifications since the company was founded in Michael Dell's dorm room.

There are various producers of products built to order – from Levi Straus and Anderson Windows to Hewlett-Packard and, of course, Dell Computer Corporation. In the last instance, computers have been made to customer specifications since the company was founded in Michael Dell's dorm room. Since that time, Dell computers have been made not only according to what a customer wants but what he or she *exactly* wants. As Dell tells visitors to its Web site (Dell.com), Dell was founded on a single concept: "that by selling personal computer systems directly to customers, Dell could best understand their needs, and efficiently provide the most effective computing solutions to meet those needs." (About two-thirds of Dell's sales are to large corporations, government agencies, and educational institutions, but Dell also handles orders from mid- and smaller-firms and home-PC users.) Through its direct business model, Dell offers in-person relationships with corporate and institutional customers; telephone and Internet purchasing (the latter now at $40 million daily); customized computer systems; phone and online technical support; and next-day, on-site product service. Nearly 50 percent of Dell's sales currently are Web-enabled, and about 40 percent of Dell's technical support activities and about 70 percent of its order-status transactions occur online.

Dell believes that the direct model is responsible for the terrific relationship the firm has with its customers. "And," he has said, "that creates valuable information, which in turn allows us to leverage our relationships with both suppliers and customers. Couple that information with technology, and you have the infrastructure to revolutionize the fundamental business models of major global companies."

According to Rashi Glazer, co-director of the Center for Marketing and Technology at the University of California at Berkley, Dell is a great example of how an IT company could use a SWOT analysis – a study of strengths, weaknesses, opportunities, and threats (the basics of strategic planning) to carve out a strong business strategy. In an article in *Computerworld,* Glazer notes Dell's strength in selling directly to customers, keeping costs lower than those of other hardware vendors, but its weakness in a lack of solid dealer relationships. In terms of opportunities, according to Glazer, Dell looked at the marketplace and recognized that customers increasingly valued convenience and one-stop shopping and that they knew what they wanted to purchase. Dell also saw the Internet as a powerful marketing tool. Threats were companies like IBM and Compaq which had strong brand names. The result, according to Glazer, was a strategy that included mass customization and just-in-time manufacturing (by letting customers design their own computers and custom-build systems). Dell stayed with its strength – direct sales – but offered its products on the Internet.

It is important to recognize that mass customization impacts not only how products are produced – the manufacturing process – but also the logistics system and the marketing approach. As Schonfeld observes in *Fortune*, "Mass customization could well be the organizing principle of business in this century, just as mass production was the organizing principle in the twentieth century." Certainly this has been the case for Dell, although it has had the advantage of practicing mass customization from its startup, unlike increasing numbers of companies that are copying its built-to-order model.

Certainly, Dell is an excellent blueprint for mass customization. For instance, as Dell demonstrates, building to order requires a continual dialogue with customers. In a column in *MWorld*, the membership Web site for the American Management Association, AMA's president and chief executive officer, Dr George Weathersby, points out that build to order or, if you prefer, mass customization, has been so successful for Dell as a customer-driven practice that organizations that emulate the firm in this success factor are said to be "Delling" their competitors. Weathersby also writes that he considers "Delling" more than a manufacturing approach, pointing to the need for organizational transformation to duplicate Dell's direct relationship with its customers.

Yes, Dell keeps margins up by keeping inventory down, building computers from readily available modular components. But, more important, Dell captures information from customers with sophisticated software, some of which was developed internally, some purchased from others. The software programs collect data and then quickly share the bytes of information with suppliers to rush shipments of hard drives or with internal teams on the factory floor where assemblers put parts together. Consequently, the direct-sell approach of Dell is much more than an economic model. As Dell vice-chairman Kevin Rollins said, "Our goal is to know exactly what the customer wants when he wants it."

> "Our goal is to know exactly what the customer wants when he wants it."
> – Dell vice-chairman, Kevin Rollins

Since increasingly the orders come via Dell's Web site, the collection of customer information is virtually a seamless process. Dell's goal would seem to be to streamline further the flow of quality information from customers to the company to gain greater insights into customer wants. This explains Michael Dell's love affair with the Web. At Dell Computer's inaugural DirectConnect Conference in early 1999, Michael Dell revealed the role of the Internet in his company's success and explained how other companies could also use it: "The Internet is like a weapon sitting on a table ready to be picked up by either you or your competitors."

Many of the reporters at the conference believed that Dell's remarks were more than a marketing pitch – rather, he was sharing his company's plans for the future. Joe Marengi, manager of Dell's corporate sales division, told the press corps, "What we're looking at is how Dell becomes an Internet company that sells into the IT space, rather than an IT-selling company that happens to use the Net." This would seem to make sense as we see the electronic industry evolve. While worldwide sales of PCs continue to rise, consumers are purchasing cheaper PCs and/or ditching their PCs for other electronic gizmos that speed Internet access. *Fortune* writer Daniel Roth quotes Micron Electronics CEO Joel Kocher, formerly head of worldwide marketing and sales for Dell, "I've lived through a world where the PC was the center of the universe. But, today, customers are putting a heck of a lot more value on the notion of having e-commerce capabilities and high-quality Web sites than they are on the box. It's no longer, 'Whose box am I going to buy and how fast is it?' "

Although Dell's actions on the Web will be explored in greater detail in Chapter 5 of this book ("Market Innovate"), the close relationship between Dell's built-to-order strategy and activities on the Web demands mention here. This closeness was evident as early as 1994 when Dell launched Dell.com. At first, the site only provided technical-support information but shortly there were price guides on the site that let customers know how much it would cost to mix and match various components for their built-to-order PCs.

By 1996, Dell.com was marketing laptops, desktops, and servers on the same site, bringing in around $1 million in revenue daily. By the end of 1999, the site had two million visitors a month, about 80 percent fewer visitors than Amazon.com, the popular e-tail site, but selling more than $30 million in products daily, ten times that of Amazon.com. More than an extremely profitable channel, the Internet has also enabled the firm to reduce sales, general, and administrative costs – from 15 percent of 1995 revenues to an estimated 9 percent in 1999.

Dell sees an opportunity to cut costs further, by 50 percent. And he's likely to do so. In 1999, Dell.com introduced a new feature that lets corporate purchases made online flow directly into customer's accounting systems. Says Ford Motor Co. CIO James A. Yost, "We can interact much, much more efficiently with them than with their rivals,"

To ensure an efficient and speedy process, the site also has links with its top 30 suppliers. The result: Dell has a return on invested capital (ROIC) of 260 percent or four times that of its best competitor. And Dell isn't done yet. Michael Dell has a concept called "e-service" that would allow hardware to automatically diagnose its problems and notify a service rep over the net.

A visit to Dell.com shows that Dell has an impressive Web presence – including pages for Dell's corporate and government clients that allow these clients to track orders, get technical help, view past orders, even know when Dell plans to introduce the next version of a specific model. The site itself runs on servers built by Dell, a fact that Dell Computer Corporation and its founder flaunt to corporate and institutional clients.

Dell.com is reportedly powered by 350 Dell PowerEdge servers powered by Intel Pentium III Xeron processors and Dell PowerVault storage systems. The operating system is Microsoft Windows NT Server 4.0 with Microsoft Internet Information Server 4.0. The Web e-commerce software is Microsoft Site Server 3.0 Commerce Edition. The database server is Microsoft SQL Server 7.0. How does Dell.com ensure the latest information on its site? Dell.com operates in a distributed environment where new information can be created on a new server, the server can be added to the network, and the distribution system can be alerted to the newest addition in less than an hour. Dell uses a distribution scheme that balances Web traffic by feeding incoming Web requests through one of many front-end PowerEdge servers, enabling additional servers to be added without impacting online operations (over a 12-month period, the site was down between seven and eight minutes). It also ensures that customers can access the information they want – such as price and model configurations – quickly, without too long a wait.

At present, Dell keeps only six days of inventory on site.

Because corporate and institutional clients are prime market for Dell, they have special pages on the site, called "Premium Pages." Similarly (according to Daniel Roth, writing in *Fortune*), suppliers have their version at the password-protected site Valuechain.Dell.com. Suppliers are being encouraged to use the site for data on how they conform to Dell standards, what orders they have shipped, and the best way to ship. The objective is to link Premier Pages to Valuechain so that as customers enter their orders a supplier will see immediately what it needs to ship Dell. At present, Dell keeps only six days of inventory on site (see Chapter 2, "Value and Manage Inventory").

THE DELL MODEL

Michael Dell has been meeting with executives – one could suggest that they represent future corporate partners – sharing the benefits of the Dell Direct Model. What is it about this sales approach?

◆ *Pay for performance.* Since Dell sells directly to customers – individuals and corporate and institutional clients – and not

PLAYING MICHAEL DELL'S GAME

If the direct model is truly the foundation of Michael Dell's Dell Computer Corporation, why can't companies like IBM, Compaq, and Hewlett-Packard duplicate his success? This point is discussed in the March–April 2000 issue of *Business Horizons* by two associate professors at University of Victoria, Victoria, BC, Canada: F. Ian Stuart (supply chain and quality management,), and David McCuthceon (operations management). They suggest that it may be easy to duplicate some supply management issues – like lower production costs of the supplies, improved conformance quality, and material/location substitution – but that lower transaction costs (think "virtual integration") may be a cost advantage that can be sustained.

In their article entitled "The Manager's Guide to Supply Chain Management," the two professors weren't talking about Dell, but the statement would seem to apply to Dell. Specifically, the two educators cited selection decisions and supply management practices in their statement that such transaction cost advantages could be sustained. They wrote, "Some gains result from securing the best suppliers – those that continue to innovate, strive for high quality levels, and routinely drive out waste. Others come from the way the firm interrelates with the supplier and how the two companies interact."

Maybe the two professors are right, but several of Dell's major competitors are trying to compete on its terms. As early as 1997, computer firms Compaq, IBM, and Hewlett-Packard were looking into how they could duplicate Dell's efficient distribution system. Compaq, for instance, has what it calls the optimized-distribution model that means PCs will be built as orders come in. For about 80 percent of all corporate orders, Compaq will customize PCs in its own plants and ship them directly. For smaller and more complex orders – about 20 percent of its shipments – Compaq will deliver half-finished PCs and leave final assembly and configuration to resellers.

Is Dell uneasy about his competitors' actions? Not at all. In a live Web broadcast in summer 1998 with Dell customers, Michael Dell was asked if he felt he could sustain his company's current market position. He told his audience that his direct business model was always evolving. "The Internet provides a great way to improve the relationship with our customers and suppliers and lower the cost at the same time." Besides, he went on, if his firm's competitors were to try to fully emulate Dell's model, they might very easily alienate resellers, the foundation for their distribution chains. While he is reportedly friendly and soft-spoken, when it comes to talking about his competitors, one reporter (Andrew E. Serwer, "Michael Dell Turns the PC World Inside Out," Fortune, September 8, 1997,) thought him to be ruthless. Of IBM, he said, according to Serwer, "There's no real momentum there." On Apple, he commented: "We're taking huge chunks of the education market from them." About Gateway, Dell reportedly said at an annual shareholders' meeting, "They're focused on first-time users. How many first-time users will there be in the year 2010?" And about Compaq, Dell said, "It's like we're the best baseball player (think "direct model") and Compaq is the best basketball player (think retail sales). "Now they want to play baseball." "The inference," Serwer writes, "is that Compaq will fare no better than Michael Jordan did when he tried his hand at hardball – and quit after batting just .202 for the minor-league Birmingham Barons."

Clearly, there's lots of rivalry between Dell and Compaq, whose headquarters are located only 160 miles apart.

through resellers, it can offer more powerful, more robust systems at less cost than its competitors.

◆ *Customization*. Customers get what they want – as I said, *exactly* what they want.

◆ *Service and support*. Information from customers via the direct model gives Dell knowledge before and after the sale to provide top quality customer service.

◆ *Latest technology*. Dell knows what its customers want. When the market shifts, Dell can quickly shift with it because its inventory turns over in eight or fewer days.

BIBLIOGRAPHY

Collett, Stacy, "SWOT Analysis," *Computerworld,* July 19, 1999.

Dell, Michael and Fredman, Catherine, *Direct from Dell: Strategies That Revolutionized an Industry*, HarperBusiness, New York 1999.

Frederick, Jim, "Compaq vs. Dell: Will Adopting Its Rival's Ways Boost Compaq's PC Fortunes?" *Money,* January 1999.

Gilmore, James H. and Pine, H.B. Joseph, "The Four Faces of Mass Customization," *Harvard Business Review,* January–February 1997.

Ladendorf, Kirk, "Dell Computer Works to Improve Custom Assembly Process," *Knight-Ridder/Tribune Business News*, September 28, 1998.

Oleson, John D. *Pathways to Agility: Mass Customization in Action*, John Wiley & Sons, New York 1998.

Pine, B. Joseph II, *Mass Customization: The New Frontier in Business Competition*, Harvard Business School Press, Boston, MA 1999.

Roth, Daniel, "Dell's Big Act," *Fortune,* December 6, 1999.

Schonfeld, Erick, "The Customized, Digitized, Have-It-Your-Way Economy," *Fortune,* September 28, 1998.

Two

GET RID OF INVENTORY

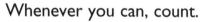

Whenever you can, count.

– Scientist and Explorer, Sir Francis Galton

Inventory management is vital to improving a company's customer service, cash flow, and ultimately its profitability. In short, inventory management or rather effective management and control of inventory can determine profitability. Inventory management is something that Dell excels at. It is a byproduct of the direct-sell approach that has been with Dell since its founding, but its worth has been so recognized that efforts are continually being made to turn inventory around even faster. Dell once told the press, "When the company started, I don't think we knew how far the direct model could take us. Most important, the direct model has allowed us to leverage our relationships with both suppliers and customers to such an extent that I believe it's fair to think of our companies as being virtually integrated."

TRADE "TRADE"

"Virtual integration" is the label that Michael Dell has given to his firm's approach of selling to individual customers and of building products in ways that harness the economic benefits of a tightly coordinated supply chain, providing information not only about customer demands but *changing* customer demands. In a speech to business leaders in Vienna, Virginia, Dell observed how:

> ... technologies available today boost the value of information sharing. We can share design databases and methodologies with not only customers but suppliers that just weren't possible five

years ago. This speeds time-to-market dramatically and creates value ... At the heart of this change is a shift away from the things we have learned to value in the business and economic models of the twentieth century.

Dell identified three changes that he saw as evidence of the move from vertical to virtual integration:

◆ the value of inventory is being replaced by the value of information;

◆ physical assets are being traded for intellectual assets; and

◆ closed business systems are giving way to collaborative relationships (see Chapter 5, "Market Innovate" and Chapter 9, "Ally with Suppliers").

All three relate to Dell's direct-sell model and, in turn, its approach to inventory management and supplier relationships. At a meeting with executives in Las Vegas in Spring 1999, Dell, once again defining his company's competitive value, observed, "I believe there's an inverse correlation between the amount of information you have and how many assets you need." The more perfect information a company has about what its customers want to buy, he said, the less need it has for physical assets in the way of inventory to supply that want. So Dell's company has found. From its information-sharing with both customers and suppliers, it has reduced its inventory needs to ten percent of those of its competitors.

In his book *The Market-Driven Organization: Understanding, Attracting, and Keeping Valuable Customers*, George S. Day, director of the Huntsman Center for Global Competition and Innovation at the Wharton School of the University of Pennsylvania, points to three elements of successful market-driven organizations. Using Dell, among others, as examples, Davis points to "distinctive capabilities in market sensing" and "a configuration that enables the entire organization continually to anticipate and respond to changing customer requirements and market conditions" as key factors, in addition to a corporate culture that recognizes the competitive advantage of providing superior customer value (see Chapter 8, "Ally with Employees"). Day observes that "market-driven firms are better educated about their markets" and consequently they are better able to form close relationships with valued customers.

In Dell's case, direct sell means that it is continually acquiring information from customers to let it anticipate and respond rapidly to changing customer requirements and market conditions. Dell has implemented sophisticated information-gathering systems, enabling it to capture customer information (as varied as leads, profiles, interactions, profile histories, and so forth) and make it immediately accessible both to internal groups (R&D, sales, customer-order management, and technical support) and outside (suppliers).

FORECAST ACCURATELY

Excessive inventory occurs because items have been bought before they are needed. It is usually uncertainty or fear of being caught short that is responsible for unneeded stocks. Dell suffers neither problem since its direct-sell approach enables it to keep close track of inventory velocity – that is, how fast various parts provided by suppliers can be turned into computers, then moved out the door to at-home PC users and corporate and institutional clients.

At Dell, every computer part carries a printed four-digit code. At the point of assembly, the part is checked to determine the time it took to go from supplier to finished personal computer. The elapsed time is called "inventory velocity." This figure is monitored since the greater the velocity, the smaller the inventory. Further, in the volatile PC marketplace, a firm like Dell Computer Corporation could get stuck with parts it no longer needs, a situation that actually occurred at Dell in 1995. As Michael Dell describes in his book *Direct from Dell*, in 1989 the company was experiencing a tremendous growth spurt. It was what Dell wanted and, in his enthusiasm to fill ever-increasing demand, he bought lots of parts – among them, memory chips – "as many as we could get our hands on." What happened? The market shifted. Prices plummeted. Even worse, the marketplace went from wanting 256K to 1 megabyte almost overnight. Recalled Dell: "We were stuck with too many chips that nobody wanted – not to mention the fact that they had cost us a ton of money." Without the kind of supplier network it has now, this was hard on the fledgling firm. It had to sell off the inventory, plunging earnings to a penny per share in one quarter. To survive, the company had to raise product prices, which slowed growth. International growth was also delayed.

> **"We were stuck with too many chips that nobody wanted – not to mention the fact that they had cost us a ton of money."**
> **– Michael Dell**

The experience reshaped Dell's thinking not only about the need to manage rapid growth but also the value and importance

THE POWER OF VIRTUAL INTEGRATION

Speaking to a group of executives in Vienna, Virginia, Michael Dell shared his fourfold concept of virtual integration, at the heart of his own company, and which he considers "a competitive imperative" for every company today:

◆ Establish direct relationships that close the gap between customer, manufacturer and supplier.
◆ Be clear about your organization's value-add. "Create partnerships for capital-intensive and labor-intensive services, and keep your own focus on doing what you do best."
◆ Choose "best-of-breed partners" and make them part of your business if they will comply with the same performance standards and quality measurements that you use within your own organization.
◆ Consider the Internet an integral part of your company's strategy, not just a new distribution channel or marketing tool. In particular, look at how it will allow you to cross traditional company-to-company boundaries logistically to improve product quality, cut inventory and thereby operating costs, increase inventory velocity, speed product delivery, and increase the total customer experience.

Other comments from Michael Dell on virtual integration have included:

◆ "For Dell, virtual integration has been a natural evolution of our business system."
◆ "While Dell has always been a company focused on process as much as technology innovation, the internet is turbo-charging the way we do business – and expediting our virtual integration."
◆ "There is an inverse correlation between the amount of information you have and how many assets [think 'inventory']."

of managing inventory. It was more than a matter of competitive advantage – it was a matter of survival. Consequently, Dell was speaking from experience when he told *Harvard Business Review:* "Inventory carries risk. If the cost of materials goes down to 50 percent in a year, and you have two to three months of inventory versus eleven days, you've got a big cost disadvantage." This makes competition based on price pretty dicey.

MONITOR INVENTORY VELOCITY

Dell monitors weekly inventory velocity and number of days of total inventory. Both figures are calculated by product and component, and shared with Dell's entire management team. Since Dell began to market via the Web, inventory velocity, already far faster than the firm's competitors, has further increased. In 1997, Dell inventory velocity was 7 days, with a total inventory at 13 days, compared with 75–1000 days for competitors that sell via retail stores. In 1998, since use of the Internet for order taking, inventory velocity was down to three days, with total inventory at seven days, versus 80 or more days for the organization's competitors. Inventory levels and new parts needs are constantly relayed via the Web. Some vendors are in communication with Dell every hour. As Dell told a reporter, the key challenge has been to change the attention of Dell's management away from how much inventory there is toward how fast it is moving. Inventory turnover is clearly a competitive advantage – and not only due to savings that can be passed along to customers in lower prices.

Yes, indeed, Dell's inventory velocity means Dell products can be sold at better prices. But it also means that there are funds for research and development and other internal investments that make the firm more competitive. It also allows Dell to address sudden change. For instance, it ensures that Dell can reduce price when the cost of parts drops substantially, something competitors with large inventories have a hard time doing. Likewise, when new hardware, software, or other technology appears, Dell, as a low-inventory firm, is able to retool more rapidly than its high-inventory competitors. As Michael Dell once explained, "If I've got 11 days of inventory and my competitor has 80, and Intel comes out with a new 450-megahertz chip, that means I'm going to get to market 69 days sooner." This is a problem companies in the volatile computer industry must regularly consider. In Dell's opinion, his firm's direct model, combined with inventory and supplier chain management, has "virtually eliminated it."

> **"If I've got 11 days of inventory and my competitor has 80, and Intel comes out with a new 450-megahertz chip, that means I'm going to get to market 69 days sooner."**
> **– Michael Dell**

Dell proudly tells his corporate customers, "We know when our customers are ready to move on technologically, and we can get out of the market beforehand." Customers don't have to suffer for their supplier's blindness to an evolving market by paying higher prices for their supplier's products.

Finally, because it turns over inventory in as few as seven days, Dell isn't likely to find itself overstocked to the point that it has to sell off excess inventory at below-market prices to make room in overstocked warehouses.

DESIGN FOR INVENTORY MANAGEMENT

Dell's success at increasing inventory velocity isn't due exclusively to its direct-sell model or partnership with its suppliers, although they clearly play a major part. It also is a reflection of product design. At Dell, products are designed to maximize inventory velocity. For instance, products for the largest part of the market are designed to have the fewest number of parts. Systems are reconfigured to allow for a limited variety of expensive parts but a greater variety of low-cost parts. The intent is to reduce the number of components to manage and thereby increase inventory velocity as well as the risk of inventory depreciation. Dell also sequences all production activities in such a way that in-process material continually moves toward the completed product.

Hydraulic tools and conveyors lift in-process material between production areas, reducing by half the time that staff touch the products.

At Dell's Metric 12 facility in Austin, its "showcase" plant, this process, known as "flow manufacturing," is complemented by a high level of automation. Hydraulic tools and conveyors lift in-process material between production areas, reducing by half the time that staff touch the products. This reduces the likelihood of damage and need for product rework.

Rework is minimized, anyhow, through a stringent quality-control process that begins at supplier facilities. There, Dell conducts regular on-site audits as well as quick, diagnostic tests during assembly. For circuit boards and other key parts, Dell directly links to suppliers' manufacturing databases, allowing it to locate glitches before parts even reach Dell plants.

So Dell is able to practice just-in-time (JIT) inventory management. To date, it has reduced cycle time for PCs – for instance from order to shipment – to three and a half days. But at Dell, that isn't enough. According to Keith Maxwell, vice-president of procurement and manufacturing, Dell's goal is to work with suppliers to figure out how to minimize the supply chain and hold the least amount of inventory in it. The more suppliers understand Dell's business, the fewer will be the "buffers" that translate into inventory. And, said Maxwell, inventory management problems can mean higher costs, poor quality or slow production, and a negative reputation for delivery time.

PRACTICE TWO-TIER JIT INVENTORY MANAGEMENT

Most of Dell's commodity suppliers have established parts warehouses near Dell plants. Manufacturing facilities are located in Austin and a suburb of Nashville (US), Limerick (Ireland) and Penang (Malaysia). Each of these facilities produces PCs on a JIT basis. To ensure smooth product flow, the company has different sourcing arrangements and delivery schedules for custom and commodity parts. Printed circuit board assemblies may be built with commodity parts but they often are uniquely assembled so PC orders can vary. Consequently, Dell sources these parts on a regional basis, receiving daily deliveries at each of its manufacturing facilities from supplier plants located in the same region. On the other hand, for commodity parts that don't need much customization (like floppy disk drives, keyboards, or power supplies), Dell has global contracts with a few suppliers, thereby allowing for better pricing and service.

Suppliers own the inventory until it is received by Dell and are expected to maintain adequate stock levels, picking parts as needed, which can be on an hourly basis.

In the past, Dell would fax or phone its requirements to suppliers who packaged the parts into reusable bins with kanban cards attached. Today, the same messages are sent over special Web pages of dell.com. Trucks then deliver the parts to the nearby plant, a continuous process that has come to be known as "the milk run." Once at the plant, the sorted parts are ready for final assembly. So Dell is further freed from having to manage inventories and the costs associated with them.

Yes, the procedure does push inventory down the supply chain, but Dell keeps suppliers from getting stuck with much inventory. Dell allows suppliers to participate in a "revolver program" where they can sell parts stored at the warehouse to other customers.

DON'T SIT ON YOUR LAURELS

Maxwell sees Dell's supply chain system (see Chapter 9, "Ally with Suppliers") as "pulling" parts from suppliers just as they are needed. In the longer term, Maxwell told a reporter that Dell is considering consolidating all production part inventories into a single "supplier logistics center" that will be managed by a third-party. As Maxwell told a reporter, "Today, having revolver sites spread around, we're pulling more deliveries and tying up dock space. Having a third-party manage parts from different suppliers in a single facility will allow us to deal with a single truck with multiple parts in it. It will also reduce our suppliers' costs, so they don't have to manage the inventory for us."

Maxwell says that Dell also hopes to have its suppliers, via special pages on Dell's Web site, share ideas for process improvements as well as traditional production, quality, and technical information. Over the longer term, Dell would like to remove all parts inventory from its supply chain by having suppliers on their own build-to-order programs. Said Maxwell, "When a customer calls with an order (for a PC), I want to have (disk-drive maker) Western Digital start building a hard drive for me and Intel start to build a motherboard for me. Our goal is to work with our suppliers."

INVENTORY MANAGEMENT À *LA* MICHAEL DELL

If Michael Dell decides one day to set up training programs for the rest of the world in "virtual integration" based on his firm's direct-sell model, he is likely to stress these points during the first class:

◆ Increase inventory velocity. Admittedly, Dell has a huge Web site that allows for the exchange of lots of information – from and to customers and suppliers – but most companies have information about their customers' wants and needs that they fail to include in inventory management.

◆ Incorporate concern about inventory management into product design. Inventory management isn't simply a purchasing issue.

◆ Develop a partnership with suppliers so that they assemble and stock much of your inventory and deliver as needed.

◆ Good isn't good enough. If you haven't incorporated the Internet into your business yet, you may be too late already. At the very least, rethink your business to see how it could give you more information about customer wants or market shifts or better your relationship with suppliers and subsequently reduce inventory and/or speed inventory velocity.

BIBLIOGRAPHY

Boulton, Richard E.S., Libert, Barry D. and Samek, Steve M., *Cracking the Value Code: How Successful Businesses Are Creating Wealth in the New Economy*, HarperBusiness, New York 2000.

Day, George S., *The Market-Driven Organization: Understanding, Attracting and Keeping Valuable Customers*, The Free Press, New York 1999.

Dell, Michael and Fredman, Catherine, *Direct from Dell: Strategies That Revolutionized an Industry*, HarperBusiness, New York 1999.

Minahan, Tim, "JIT: A Process with Many Faces," *Purchasing*, September 4, 1997.

Naumann, Earl, *Creating Customer Value: The Path to Sustainable*

Competitive Advantage, International Thomson Publishing, Cincinnati, OH 1995.

Wheeler, Steven and Hirsch, Evan, *The Channel Advantage: How Top Companies Connect with Their Customers*, Jossey-Bass, San Francisco 1999.

Wild, Tony, *Best Practice in Inventory Management*, John Wiley & Sons, Inc., New York 1997.

Three

LOVE YOUR SUPPLIERS ...

Business is about communications, sharing data, and instantaneous decision-making. If you have on your desk a device that enables you to communicate and share data with your colleagues around the world, you will have a strategic advantage.
– Andrew S. Grove

J ust as Dell's direct model is increasing customer contact and insights – now primarily online, through the Internet, and initially via phone and fax – so it is also growing and nurturing supplier relationships. Many organizations claim they are customer-focused, giving customers the products they want in the manner they want them. But to do that, it truly isn't sufficient to:

◆ *Understand customer needs.* This is only one step in the process.

◆ *Restructure the organization and redo the policies to respond rapidly to customer wants.* Once again, it is only the beginning. While it is important to develop internal systems to support sales efforts, it is not enough.

◆ *Set up information systems.* Yes, we need to track customer orders and maintain information on our own inventory velocity. But such measurements and record-keeping are, again, only a small part of the customer equation.

SO WHAT IS MISSING?

To be a truly customer-driven organization, serving customers the way they want to be served, an organization must integrate its internal logistics systems with those of its suppliers. A customer-focused company has to be very much a relationship-oriented organization, as Dell is, according to its founder. And this goes beyond good customer relations. The company's supply chain is very much based on building a strong relationship with each and every one of its major and minor suppliers. Initially, those contacts were by phone. Today, they are facilitated online, from a special Web site maintained for all its suppliers. Currently 24 suppliers provide almost 85 percent of its materials.

"We have put a big X through traditional manufacturing." – Michael Dell

Dell told a reporter, "We have put a big X through traditional manufacturing. We focus on how fast we can deliver product, and we have designed manufacturing to be a continuous flow with customer specific aspects such as loading proprietary customer software built into the process." Writing in *Industry Week,* reporter Michael A. Verespej quotes Dell as saying, "To have high levels of raw materials or finished goods in a warehouse can be very dangerous in a business where the value of these materials is going down about 1 percent a week." Verespez adds, "That inventory obsession has reduced the dollar volume of inventories at Dell by 15 percent in the last 21 months even as sales have risen sevenfold."

MAKE THE SUPPLY CHAIN PART OF THE VALUE CHAIN

Dell hasn't just contracted with its suppliers; it has allied with them. And the result has been speedier delivery, shipment of the newest and best technology, and top-quality service to customers. In short, Dell's approach to its suppliers supports the firm's effort to maximize "the total customer experience."

THE PRINCIPLES OF VIRTUAL INTEGRATION

If you dig deep into Dell.com, you will find several speeches delivered by Michael Dell from 1998 through 1999. Most have to do with his effort to leverage the Web to continue rapid growth for his firm. But one speech addresses "Collaboration in a Connected Economy: the Power of Virtual Integration," delivered in Vienna, Virginia, in June of 1998. In that presentation, Dell identified three factors that have changed as his organization has shifted from vertical integration to virtual integration via greater communication with customers and suppliers through the Internet:

◆ the replacement of the value of inventory with the value of information;
◆ the exchange of physical assets for intellectual assets; and
◆ the creation of collaborative relationships instead of closed business systems.

Dell told his audience that as industries mature, product differentiation becomes more difficult. Instead, process innovation must take its place as a means of competitive advantage. Such process innovations in time, he continued, would blur traditional boundaries between suppliers and manufacturers and manufacturers and customers. The result will be shrinkage of both time and distance in delivery of products to customers.

Dell suggested four principles that firms need to follow to emulate Dell's success with virtual integration:

1. Establish direct relationships that close the gap between customer, manufacturer and supplier.

2. Determine your company's value-add very specifically. Further, said Dell, "Create partnerships for capital-intensive and labor-intensive services, and keep your own focus on doing what you do best." In talking about labor-intensive services, Dell wasn't only referring to supplier relationships but use of outside services to handle telemarketing.

3. Develop relationships with top quality producers. Dell used the term "best-of-breed partners." It's imperative, he said, that companies that practice virtual integration hold their suppliers to the same performance standards and quality metrics that they employ in their own business.

4. Consider the Internet an integral part of your company's strategy. As Dell observed, only when you think of the Web as a part of your corporate strategy can you use it to cross-traditional company-to-company (think "customer and supplier") boundaries and thereby truly achieve virtual integration.

Dell went on to explain to his audience how virtual integration had been a natural evolution of its own direct model, selling personal computer systems directly to customers. This meant that early in its history it had partnered for capital-intensive services with suppliers, placing corporate attention, instead, on delivering customer-directed solutions. Consequently, early on, Dell said, his firm was able to gain the benefits of a tightly coordinated supply chain. Running a vertically integrated business enabled it to achieve the core competencies of speed and flexibility. But, he said, "the Internet is turbo-charging the way we do business – and expediting our virtual integration." To date, Dell makes 50 percent or so of its sales via the Web. But at the time of this keynote address Dell was able to point to sales of about $1 million a day from Dell.com, global sales exceeding $5 million, and an expected annual sales figure of $2 billion.

He suggested, however, that use of the Internet as a sales channel was only a small part of its ultimate value to doing business. "The real potential of the Internet lies in its ability to transform relationships with the traditional supplier-vendor-customer chain." Dell then went on to describe how his firm, with special links to suppliers and customers, is able to speed information flow, thereby saving both time and money. "It transforms organizations by eliminating paper-based functions, flattening organizational layers, and integrating global operations seamlessly," he told the business audience. "By virtually integrating with our suppliers," he said, "we literally bring them into our business. And because our entire production is build-to-customer order, it requires dynamic and tight inventory control. By working virtually with Dell, we challenge our suppliers to reach new heights of quality and efficiency. This improves *their* process and their inventory control, which creates greater value for them, as well as for Dell." The shift from physical assets such as inventory to information assets such as the Premium Pages for customer firms and Web links for suppliers has, just as importantly, created massive benefits for the firm's shareholders and employees.

He concluded his presentation with these words of advice: "I have chosen to describe the way that Dell is using virtual integration not because I want to promote Dell but because I believe that virtual integration is an extraordinarily powerful means of organizing businesses."

DO WHAT YOU ARE GOOD AT DOING

From the beginning, Dell didn't buy the components for its computers – it didn't have the cash. But, then, there was also no reason to do so since there were companies already out there doing that. Dell, instead, chose to focus on its customers, designing and delivering the systems they wanted. Contrary to fear that dependence on outside suppliers could lose a business control over the manufacturing end of its business, Dell found that it could actually gain greater control over product quality. Its secret? Its choice of suppliers.

Dell has made it a practice to choose from among the best to supply its parts. The goal is to identify for each and every part or component the expertise and experience to produce a high-quality part or component. If a smaller but quality supplier can't keep up with demand, Dell works to pair the first supplier with a second to handle inventory needs. To ensure the quality it demands, Dell makes clear that its suppliers understand its expectations.

Before putting signature to contract, Dell meets with supplier representatives to give a clear idea of its requirements – from design objectives to delivery and logistics, to service, to global requirements and, finally, to costs. In particular, Dell sees that its suppliers have a clear understanding of the direct model and importance of inventory velocity – and not only to Dell. As suppliers learn more about the direct model, Dell has told the press, they gain a real appreciation of its value not only to Dell but to them as well. Because the direct model provides ongoing feedback from customers, Dell gets insights into customer needs and wants which it shares with its suppliers. So Dell's suppliers are often ahead of their own competitors about what the market wants and doesn't want, enabling them to adjust their own output and resolve problems with existing parts. Dell has told representatives from client firms, "Depending on our assessment, we can tell our suppliers where the market is heading. This allows them to align their product mix with customer demand, which, in turn, improves the efficiency and velocity of both their inventory and ours."

AVOID COMPLEXITY

Initially, Dell had around 40 different suppliers. Growth led to the addition of more suppliers. But as the number grew and began to make manufacturing logistics more difficult, not to mention add to operational costs, the firm chose to reduce the number back to around 40 and currently it is at 25, representing 85 percent of all materials.

PROXIMITY PAYS

Dell is a global company with plants in the US, Ireland, Malaysia, and China. Consequently, its suppliers must also be global – indeed, their plants must be located near enough to Dell plants to keep shipping down, both in time and costs. Consequently, if you plan to continue to supply parts to Dell, you have to be prepared to build your plants near new Dell plants. Michael Dell tells the story of one supplier that wanted to keep Dell as a customer, and consequently constructed a plant in Malaysia near the plant being constructed by Dell.

> "Suppliers need to have a sprint capacity to work with us."
> – Michael Dell

Obviously, Dell's suppliers have to be willing to adapt to Dell's expansion plans. But when Michael Dell talks about supplier flexibility, he speaks more about its flexibility to respond to the marketplace's demands. "It's incumbent upon us to see that our partners [think "suppliers"] respond to market demand so that we'll all succeed." He continues, "Suppliers need to have a sprint capacity to work with us." In other words, Dell suppliers have to have the finances to increase their production capacity to meet Dell's needs. If the market shifts interest in one kind of offering to another or a technology evolves, a Dell supplier has to have the manufacturing capacity – and investment dollars – to adapt with the market in order to accommodate Dell's new needs. Actually, Dell shares its three-year capacity plan with its suppliers and they, in turn, have to describe their current production capacity and plans to expand as well.

Dell treats his firm's suppliers as allies, even associates ("like a part of the company"). Because of Dell's direct model and inventory velocity, it needs to share daily production requirements. Dell has told the press, "We have replaced the traditional 'bid-buy' cycle with a relationship based on ongoing communications and a huge amount of shared information."

MONITOR QUALITY

A Dell advertisement points up the importance to Dell of nitpicking customers because they keep the organization on its toes. Dell has the same attitude about its relationship with its suppliers. It has formalized the process with a supplier report card that compares actual performance against standards like number of defects per million. Today, many organizations measure their employees' and managers' performance via a 360-degree feedback assessment. Dell sees its report card as a 360-degree evaluation, tracking individual supplier's performance against its expectations (not only in delivery and manufacture but field operation) and the supplier's competitors for purposes of comparison. The goal for Dell is fewer

WHAT FACTORS DOES DELL MONITOR?

In terms of corporate measurements, it uses the balance sheet and the fundamentals of the P&L on a monthly basis as tools to manage operations. From the balance sheet, Dell has said the company tracks three cash-flow measurements closely: weekly updates of how many days of inventory the firm has, broken out by product components; receivables; and payables. "This is basic blocking and tackling, but we give them high priority," he has said. "The payoff is that we have a negative cash-conversion cycle of five days." What does that mean? It means that Dell gets paid for its products before it has to pay its suppliers!

How does this compare with Dell's competitors? They have to support their resellers by offering them credit. Consequently, virtual integration based on the direct model gives Dell a tremendous cost advantage. The shorter the cash-collection cycle, the greater the competitive advantage.

In terms of P&L, Dell watches most closely its margins, its average selling price, and the overhead associated with selling.

than 1000 defects per million of finished computer systems, a high standard indeed since it means that individual components can only have a defect rate of 0.00001 percent.

Suppliers receive regular feedback from Dell on how they are meeting the quantitative measures for success set by Dell. This helps suppliers, in turn, with their own quality control programs. Dell has referred to this as a "self-enforcing checks and balance system."

WHAT ABOUT THE STANDARDS BY WHICH SUPPLIERS ARE HELD?

In the beginning, Dell set up tough processes to ensure quality performance, from designing for reliability to manufacturing for field performance. A phase review process enabled it to ensure that products wouldn't move along on the assembly line unless they passed quality and performance at each stage of development. Continuous improvements of methodologies led to considerable awards for system performance and reliability. But Web-based links (virtual integration) have meant that the firm can now take quality measurements to greater detail.

Dell had long had supplier certification programs through which Dell suppliers must pass tough periodic evaluations to be sure that quality meets Dell standards. Previously Dell suppliers had periodic evaluations. Now, courtesy of the Web links, suppliers regularly receive online metrics of their performance by region, line of business, and customer feedback. Besides, components that don't meet Dell standards are returned to suppliers – Dell has said that means his firm's suppliers "have their own skin in the game" courtesy of its "direct return initiative."

According to Dell, over a fifteen-month period, courtesy of the Web links, quality of components increased 40 percent. So pleased is the company with the results to date that Dell says its future goal is to apply the same kind of rigid quality controls over the vendors to its suppliers.

Dell told reporters, "You have to be self-critical to succeed," referring as much to himself as to his firm's suppliers. At Dell's management meetings, he has told his peers, you would find a "remarkably self-critical bunch with a disdain for complacency ... We are always looking to do things better." When problems arise, Dell has said, he and his management team look to how they can redesign operations so it doesn't recur. This search for greater efficiency isn't limited to the manufacturing plant, either. Consider Dell.com. Word has it that his management executives were skeptical but Dell himself pushed the idea of selling computers directly from his firm's Web site, evolving his "direct model" to an "Internet direct model" over time.

PRACTICE DEMAND/SUPPLY, NOT SUPPLY/DEMAND

Inventory velocity is an important metric for Dell, and to achieve the kind of turnaround time for parts in its facilities that Dell's direct model demands, it needs to stay in regular communication with its suppliers. As Dell has explained to business leaders, his biggest problem was re-educating suppliers that traditionally sent large shipments to warehouses where they would remain until they were needed. That need might not be immediate – which could mean that market demands changed before the stock was used. Sometimes some of the stock, based on overly optimistic projections, was never used. The answer for Dell was to order as needed, which meant to buy less but at a faster rate. This actually would be beneficial to suppliers, as Michael Dell explained to them. "Ship us inventory every day or every hour as we need it," he recalls telling them. "We'll buy from you faster. And if you can do that, we'll buy a whole lot more."

Since this represented a major shift in supplier thinking, Dell's suppliers had to see *real* benefits to them in shifting from supply/

demand logistics, based on often unrealistic forecasts to demand/ supply logistics, based on actual needs. In essence, Dell offered to trade information on methodologies, shifting market trends, and product problems for frequent smaller deliveries of parts. Today, Dell plants maintain supplies for only a few days – for some, a few hours. Inventory levels are communicated regularly. Likewise, replenishment needs – again, sometimes hourly. Suppliers know exact production requirements.

Dell is continually searching for ways to reduce inventory – to speed inventory velocity. Indeed, at its Round Rock facility, according to one reporter, for the purpose of gaining velocity throughout the supply chain, a line of monitors is never handled by workers. There is no need to do so – so why waste the time. The supplier has surpassed Dell's metric for defects, providing reliable monitors with less than 1000 defects per million. Consequently Dell decided there was no need to take them out of the shipping cartons for testing. Actually, given the level of quality, unpacking, touching, and testing them, then repackaging them for delivery to the end user would only be risking damage to the monitors plus adding time in the plant.

> "Dell has one integrated process for managing the entire value chain, from component supplier to end customer – and we control all the aspects in-between."
> – Michael Dell

But the real secret of speeding inventory turnover is communication, as Dell learned earlier, Consequently the more communication between Dell and its suppliers, it reasoned, the more likely it could reduce inventory and shorten time and distance between supplier and customer. And what more logical way to improve communication than via the Internet? A special Web site has been created for Dell's suppliers, just as there are special sites for its corporate customers. Information is provided by Valuechain.dell.com on all aspects of the supplier relationship – from issues of quality to cost to inventory levels to order demand. "This allows us to bring our suppliers inside our business and treat them as if they were part of our company," Dell told a business meeting in summer 1999. The information is available simultaneously, in real time. For example, there is a link to Intel that allows the firm to manage quickly and efficiently order flow and just-in-time inventory delivery. Ultimately Dell hopes to link its internal management systems to suppliers overseas and their factories producing the components. Dell has told reporters, "Because of the Internet we can maintain a continuous flow of materials from our suppliers into our factories. This means our people spend less time placing orders or expediting parts and more time adding value."

Equally important, the transmission of data to suppliers directly contributes to the "total quality experience for customers." Dell gets quality data every minute of the day – from its plants and, via the direct model, its customers. That information can now be shared, as received, with suppliers. If suppliers are given a metric to meet – a standard like 500 defects per million – and they don't meet it, Dell wants to let them know immediately, not a month or quarter from then. "If we can accelerate the availability of the data, our chances of encouraging suppliers to improve also increases."

In a speech to executives in Chicago in fall 1998, Dell told the audience, "When the Internet came along as a way of contacting our customers and suppliers, it was a natural for us. We started

with providing information and eventually went into the process of selling products online, and now the Internet has
fundamentally changed the way we do business and is an integral part of our whole company strategy." Admittedly, some
executives would be squeamish about sharing what has been traditionally guarded information – capacities, capabilities, supply
inventories, component quality ratings, etc. – but Dell firmly
believes that "collaboration is the new competitive imperative."
He has told reporters, "Both suppliers and customers must be
treated as partners and collaborators, jointly looking for ways to
improve efficiency across the entire spectrum of the value chain."

MICHAEL DELL'S FORMULA FOR SOLID SUPPLIER RELATIONSHIPS

Dell's approach with suppliers is really based on common sense
(but, then, as experience demonstrates, common sense isn't as
common as it should be):

◆ *Stick to your strengths*. As you will read in future chapters, Dell
   knows not to spend critical internal resources where the same
   can be purchased. So it outsources telemarketing efforts.
   Likewise, rather than develop parts for its products, it goes
   to the best suppliers for them. Dell has exhorted, "Find out
   where you can add the most value to your customers and
   shareholders, and find great partners to do the rest." He
   has told the press, "We keep our focus on doing what we do
   best and ask ourselves what is the most efficient way to do
   things."

◆ *Simplify relationships*. Dell has learned that fewer suppliers mean fewer chances for confusion, and greater consistency in quality.

◆ *Practice virtual integration*. Yes, Dell seeks out suppliers that can not only provide quality parts but also deliver them quickly to Dell assembly facilities because they have nearby manufacturing capacity. But beyond this physical proximity, Dell now is electronically close to its suppliers on Dell.com that provides ongoing communication with suppliers.

BIBLIOGRAPHY

"Understand the Role of Customization," in *Bushed*, Harper-Business, New York 1999.

Dell, Michael, "Building the Infrastructure for the 21st Century Commerce," speech in Las Vegas, NV, May 12, 1999.

Dell, Michael, "The Dell Advantage," speech in San Francisco, March 3, 1999.

Dell, Michael, "Direct Connect," speech in Austin, Texas, August 15, 1999.

Dell, Michael, "The Dynamics of the Connected Economy," speech in Atlanta, June 25, 1999.

Dell, Michael, "NetSpeed: The Supercharged Effect of the Internet," speech in Chicago, October 23, 1998.

Elliott, Heidi, "Better, Stronger, Faster," *Electronic Business Today*, September 1997.

Magretta, Joan, "The Power of Virtual Integration: An Interview with Dell Computer's Michael Dell," *Harvard Business Review*, March–April 1998.

Sheridan, John H., "Focused on Flow," *Industry Week*, October 18, 1999.

Verespez, Michael A., "Michael Dell's Magic," *Industry Week*, November 16 1998.

Four

... BUT LOVE YOUR EMPLOYEES EVEN MORE

Amazing things happen when you make people feel they are valued as individuals, when you dignify their suggestions and their ideas, when you show your respect for them by allowing them to exercise their own wisdom and judgment and discretion.
**– Herb Kelleher, president,
Southwest Airlines**

A t Dell Computer Corporation, you have plenty of fleas and few, if any, elephants. Huh? They are metaphors that Charles Handy, the management guru, used at the 32nd Global Human Resources Conference sponsored by the American Management Association at Nice in Spring 1999 to describe two different kinds of managers and employees. Those who are fleas are those who produce ideas, who tickle the elephants, or bureaucrats, in slow-moving corporations, which Dell is certainly not. Fleas are passionate about their work, eager to make a difference – to make something happen. This may explain why they really want to do what they are doing.

How has Michael Dell managed to bring managers and employees with such commitment and enthusiasm together?

RECRUIT THE BEST

Certainly, there is a lot of competition for the kind of people that Dell needs. And Dell needs 100 new hires each week to sustain its growth.

Barbara Beck, head of HR for Cisco Systems, told a group of executives how her company found some of its key engineers and technicians. The company built a firewall to protect Cisco internal systems from hackers. But still people got through. Those people were offered jobs at Cisco. She told the group, "They would obviously be curious and interested people – exactly what we needed." Consequently, when these individuals successfully hacked into Cisco's systems, they were redirected to a page that said, 'Welcome to Cisco Systems. Would you like a job?' " Today, Cisco uses a Profiler that is basically an online CV that can be completed and sent in. But "because it takes about ten minutes to fill in," explained Beck, "and because at Cisco we like to do things in unusual ways and we believe work should be fun, we created an 'Uh, oh. My Boss Is Coming' button that allows an applicant to turn the form into something more innocent when their manager is coming." Dell's approach to recruitment has its own twist, too.

> "To prevent its growth from spinning out of control, Dell uses a strategy that splits off business segments once they reach a certain threshold,"
> – Carla Joinson, HRMagazine.

In an article in *Fast Company*, Andy Esparza, in charge of recruitment for Dell, told how there is a quiet office within Dell headquarters in which periodically a cowbell clangs. Whenever he or a colleague lands a great new hire, the bell is rung. And with cause. As an ever-growing business, finding talented people is a top priority. In 1999, for the second year in a row, the number one priority was *people*. Esparza told *Fast Company*, "There's a war for talent going on and we're right in the middle of it."

Preston Handler, a partner with Hewitt Associates, puts the total of unfilled jobs in the IT sector alone at 500,000. He expects that to rise to 1.6 million by the year 2002.

What is Dell's battle plan? Recruitment is everyone's responsibility, not only that of the 100-plus employees in recruitment. Everyone at Dell is charged with networking for talented em-

THE BASIS OF CORPORATE CULTURES

Cultures differ from one company to another, but all are a reflection of a number of common characteristics:

◆ *Synergy.* The interaction among different people creates the social environment.
◆ *Emotion.* Yes, feelings influence culture, whether they are feelings of confidence in the organization or insecurity.
◆ *History.* The organization's past creates patterns that can continue into the future. Employees, for instance, look for companies where trust and loyalty, two key components of a positive work environment, have been demonstrated not only in words but actions over a period of time.
◆ *Slogans.* Yes, actions are more important than words, but slogans can help shape an organization's culture, too. Think, for instance, of the Ford slogan: "Quality is Job #1." Not only did that make great advertising but it was a management message for all at Ford to live by.
◆ *Dynamic.* Culture is not stable; rather, it continually evolves based on actions by not only the corporate leader but management team.
◆ *Fuzzy.* Besides frenetic, sometimes culture can be unclear. If you want to make changes to your corporate culture, you need to study it carefully first to capture its essence. Only then can you work with the elements above to influence the kind of organization you want.

ployees. They have also been known to discourage those they don't think will fit well within Dell. In the case of candidates they think could contribute to Dell, they let Esparza's department know. Dell himself has been known to follow up leads himself, and Esparza described him as "a great closer."

Finding the right people for Dell – inspired, committed, passionate workers (Handy's fleas) – is an ongoing responsibility, prompted not by need to fill vacancies but the need to stay ahead of the competition by having the best people. If the company has no job for someone but wants that person, it will make a position. Often, too, there is someone within the organization overworked, and it has become almost a tradition at Dell to split jobs. When the company first did it, Dell has told the press, there was some opposition. Those whose jobs were halved felt threatened. But in time, as their responsibilities grew with the growth of the company, they looked to the time when their job once again might be split.

AN EXECUTIVE IS KNOWN BY THE COMPANY HE KEEPS

Michael Dell doesn't believe that splitting jobs is just something to do with others' jobs. He believes it makes sense for everyone within his company – himself included. And on three occasions, he has done it. The first time was in 1994. The company's information systems and management hadn't kept pace with its rapid growth, and it was becoming evident that Dell couldn't both oversee the day-to-day activities and continue to stay abreast of customer trends. He also had just lost his financial manager.

So that year, Dell chose to split his position as chairman as well as bring on a team of experienced executives to help set a pattern of management the fast-growing company needed. He chose his new senior management team from firms like Motorola, Hewlett-Packard, and Apple Computer. For instance, his new vice-chairman was Mortimer Topfer, former head of

Motorola's land mobile products division. As head of Dell's product group, he chose Eric Harslem from Apple Computer. Another Apple executive, John Medica, became head of Dell's notebook division. Richard Snyder, formerly general manager of Hewlett-Packard's DeskJet printer division, took over management of Dell's operations in North and South America. Finally, Dell acquired, as his chief financial officer, Tom Meredith, from Sun Microsystems.

The story goes that Meredith was the first to warn Dell of pending problems when he saw the firm's financials. Dubbed an "alarmist" in 1992 by Dell, by 1995 he was called "prophet". Meredith is attributed with what has become the firm's obsession with liquidity, profitability, and growth.

> Dell has identified the qualities its new employees will need by analyzing existing top-performing employees and looking for keys to their success.

This management team assisted Dell to create the current culture at the computer company. Rahul Jacob, writing for *Fortune*, quotes Synder, "I think the word is 'discipline.' It's very easy to have everything be urgent and important. But you can't be in that mode for long without burning out." Jacob continues, "The definition of discipline embraces such standard goals as meeting financial commitments all the way down the organization but it also includes the kind of soft goals emphasized at H-P, such as respect for the individual. That shift may make Dell a kinder, gentler place to work."

Some of these additions from the mid-1990s have moved on. But others have stayed, like Morton Topfer, who is now counselor to the CEO and director.

HOW DO YOU FIND GREAT EMPLOYEES?

In their book *Finding and Keeping Great Employees* (AMACOM), authors Jim Harris and Joan Brannick identify eight best practices to help find great employees. How do these fit within the Dell model?

◆ *Include a "WOW" factor.* WOW companies set themselves apart one way or another. "Not being seen as part of the crowd is a tremendous competitive advantage," write the authors. One way a company can do this is to be the fastest-growing company in the industry, right? Which is what Dell is.

◆ *Treat applicants like customers.* Esparza and other recruiters at Dell know the characteristics of their ideal applicants and they invest their resources in identifying potential hires with these characteristics, then court them in the same way that a sales person would court a major account. Both have a bottom-line value to the organization.

◆ *Play up image.* Dell's Web site demonstrates the kind of image it wants job candidates to see. It demonstrates the company's support of various local and civic causes, points to its efforts to sustain hires' employability through training and other work development, and plays up the company's reputation, as well as that of Michael Dell himself.

◆ *Get real.* Dell plays up its strengths but it also makes clear to potential recruits that working for Dell demands much, given the commitment that working for the firm demands. Consequently, hires at Dell come with open eyes to the ever-increasing workload they may have to accept.

◆ *Seek out candidates.* Dell doesn't sit and wait for candidates to come to it. It goes out and locates those that would fit within the culture and have the mindset for Dell. They then make an effort to interest them. If they don't have a position right then for someone they know could make a major contribution to the firm, they will create a job for that person. They know that if they don't hire them, someone – likely one of their competitors – will do so.

◆ *Utilize various recruiting techniques.* Not only does Dell's recruiting operation seek out new hires. It is such a high priority within the organization that every manager is expected to be on the look out for suitable candidates for Dell.

◆ *Know who they want.* Dell has researched to identify those characteristics that make for a successful Dell employee or manager and they use that research, measuring applicants against those factors of success from current and previous Dell employees.

◆ *Set the standard.* With a demand for about 100 new hires monthly to sustain its growth, Dell is continually looking for new ways to find qualified candidates for its organization. It doesn't follow the example of its competitors but rather becomes the standard for them, providing a model for other firms to emulate.

In 1997, Michael Dell split the position of chairman again, then in 1999 he did it one more time. There are now two vice-chairmen: Kevin B. Rollins and Dr. James T. Vanderslice. Rollins is responsible for worldwide sales, marketing and service, and for overseeing Dell's Worldwide Home and Small Business Group, European operations, and the Personal Systems Group. Before his appointment to his current position, he was president of Dell Americas. He is a former partner and director of Bain & Co., where he specialized in strategies and management for high-tech and consumer-product clients.

Vanderslice, vice-chairman since 1999, previously was senior vice-president and group executive for IBM's Technology Group, and a member of the company's corporate executive committee. During a 33-year career with IBM, Vanderslice led various global operations, including its communications-products division, manufacturing and development for its Asia Pacific Group, and computer-products division.

RECRUIT ON THE WEB

With this kind of senior management team, and Dell Computer Corporation's reputation, no wonder so many talented engineers and technicians want to work for the firm. About one-third of Dell's new hires come via the Dell.com site.

At the site, candidates can check for openings or they can submit their résumés. They can download an interview pack courtesy of Dell, including information on benefits; life in Austin and Lebanon, Tennessee, where the company also has manufacturing, technical, support, and sales staff; community initiatives, including The Dell Foundation, a corporate chari-

---

HOW HUMAN RESOURCES OPERATES

Segmentation even includes the human resources function at Dell, which is broken into two parts: operations and management. HR operations oversees benefits, compensation, and employee relations, through a service center. Staff members report directly up the chain through HR and rarely have contact with business units. HR management includes Dell University, the company's education and training function; staffing; and HR generalists who report to both the vice-president of a business unit and vice-president of HR. Operations deals with employees whereas management supports Dell's business, developing the division's leadership team, producing metrics for turnover, productivity, and the like, and developing an HR strategy for that line of business.

---

table foundation focused on equipping youth primarily in Texas and Tennessee for the digital economy, online employee giving program, and volunteerism that mobilizes Dell employees to address worldwide needs; its *diversity difference* program that recognizes "that our universe of differences and similarities offer a universe of possibilities and opportunities"; and finally its workforce development program that ensures that Dell top talent remain at the top of their field.

SEE YOUR EMPLOYEES HAVE THE TRAINING THEY NEED

Dell considers training critical. Given its rapid growth, it needs a workforce that can readily implement changing plans. "The

HR challenge is to get the workforce developed and ready," according to Steve Price, vice-president of human resources for Dell's Public and Americas International Group. Training goes beyond technical training to include leadership and other developmental training, as well as tuition reimbursement for outside courses. Training is provided through Dell's own corporate university, a partnership with the Graduate School of Business at the University of Texas at Austin, and of course online. Dell is very much into using technology for purposes of training. So Dell technical support people can go to a Web site before a new product is launched and learn how to fix it, as well as access other kinds of information. Sales personnel leave sales meetings with a CD-ROM containing all the information presented during the session.

To ensure that Dell employees get the training they need, HR continually re-evaluates and improves its training programs. The staff itself undergoes training each year and goes through a four-level evaluation process to see if a class can be redesigned or improved. Such assessments have led, for instance, to the redesign of the organization's new-hire orientation for its sales force, according to John Cone, vice-president of Dell University. "We not only cut off two weeks of ramp time [that is, the time it takes a new salesperson to reach 100 percent of quota] but also cut one week off the orientation."

Business units control training dollars. The decision was made in 1997 and led to lots of training disappearing but the total amount of training growing. Better, employees are able to ask for and get customized courses through their business segment.

Up-and-comers get special attention. According to Price, Dell conducts executive panel interviews with such individuals. Upon their completion, he meets with all the executives who interviewed the fast-tracker. He then sits down with that person and his or her supervisor and provides feedback. "It's a very, very grooming type of experience," Price has told the press. "People get some of the best executive feedback that they've ever gotten in their careers." This includes recommendations for training.

Dell formed a partnership at the Graduate School of Business at the University of Texas at Austin, to provide its managers with a level of executive education that it felt would not be available without such a partnership. Professors from the local university meet with Dell executives to create the curriculum for a finance program detailing the special way liquidity, growth and earnings must be balanced under the direct-sales model. "We show students how capital spending can have a significant impact on the profitability of the business – how if it gets too high it leverages in a negative direction," Stan Horner, Dell's director for executive education, told a representative from *CFO, The Magazine for Financial Executives*. In creating such a partnership, Dell is considered on the cutting edge of an executive-education trend.

"WE WANT YOU"

Dell will hire talented individuals whether a position exists or not. Michael Dell says, "We hire people for the long-term in mind. We're not bringing them in to do a job; we're inviting them to join the company." He continues that the company is looking for the kind of match in which the new hire has the potential to grow far beyond their current position, thereby adding "depth and additional capacity into your organization ... [during] the next wave of growth or the next competitive challenge." Still, the metric-based firm does monitor recruitment the same way it measures all other activities. The organization anticipates demand for workers by engaging annually in Dell's Web-based *organizational human resource planning* process, which allows for succession planning, key job identification, competency planning, and employee development.

Since most executives are unlikely to apply from the Web site, Dell's top headhunter has formed his own team to come up with potential candidates for Dell. Checking out newspapers, trade journals, and company Web sites, the group's members look for mergers, layoffs, a drop in stock value, all situations that might prompt a talented executive to be looking for a new job. Once they locate such an individual, action is swift. Candidates are immediately contacted.

Candidates needn't come from the high-tech field. Dell believes that it can teach the nuances of the computer business, but study of previous Dell success stories has identified the skills, ability, and knowledge that Dell is searching for. Based on his research, Esparza and Dell have identified five competencies for executive hires: the ability to learn fast; to thrive in a changing environment; to deliver results; to solve problems; and to build teams. Besides, they look for people who think in a manner compatible with corporate values and beliefs. Say they hire a service person. They promise to provide a superior total customer experience, yet the service person hired is short-tempered with the customer. Imagine the impression he or she leaves with the customer, regardless of the rest of the service experience with Dell. As the career pages at Dell.com make clear, Dell isn't looking for one type of person or personality. Nor does it want people who willingly will join in groupthink. Beyond recognizing the importance of Dell's customer-focus, they want people who want to use their talents, abilities, and – perhaps most of all – imagination, to the benefit of all of Dell.

Clearly Dell wants people who like challenges – whether CEOs, vice-presidents, engineers, even assembly workers. After all, in the team-based Dell, it's not unusual for managers to assemble people familiar with a problem situation and brainstorm a solution then and there. Esparza said, "What gets people excited is an environment in which we're growing our business at 40 percent a year, particularly if they're working somewhere that's flat." That's the message that Esparza sends when talking to candidates – and even their families. Dell recognizes that relocation adds to the pressure of saying "yes" to a job offer and consequently they court not only the potential executive but his or her family members. Candy, flowers, dinner with the candidate and spouse, a fast flight from Austin to where a sought manager is located – all are used to discourage second thoughts or counteroffers from current employers. All are designed to send the message that can be found on the Web site pages of Dell.com devoted to finding a career at Dell: "Dell is a unique company, from our Dell Direct Business Model to our CEO Michael Dell."

The site explains why Dell should be their choice: Dell is special because its success, it says, "directly impacts each and every employee at the company, whether through stock options, profit-sharing, incentive plans (for eligible employees), customer satisfaction, or career opportunity – even the experience of being part of the winning team." Preston Handler's research has found why people leave jobs, and they include "to take a promotion, to work for a 'hot' company, a poor work environment and poor leadership or management." He also has studied why they stay. They have the opportunity to learn new skills, they are working on the latest technology, they have a great working environment, or they believe they are under great leadership and management. All would explain not only the high recruitment rate at Dell but also high retention rate there.

HIRE PEOPLE IN SYNC WITH CORPORATE CULTURE

Dell has its own culture, and that makes it important to recruit a certain type of employee mindset. For instance, at Dell titles and levels don't mean much. Candidates can't be caught up in position. Former titles don't always correlate to those in past positions because Dell's structure is relatively flat. Further, more responsibility isn't necessarily better. Maybe from its experience in 1994, Dell will split jobs when they grow beyond the point of management. "When we take half of what you have away from you and tell you to go rebuild it, that's a sign of success," Steve Price, vice-president of human resources for Dell's *public and Americas international group*, told the press. Dell's compensation backs up this measure of success by rewarding managers who grow the business to the point that segmentation is required – that business segments reach a certain threshold and need to be split.

Dell people are more than employees – they are owners, as a result of employee stock purchase plans, stock option grants, and 401(k) plans in which employee contributions are met not with dollars but with Dell stock – and therefore Dell employees are allied in meeting Dell's strategic plans.

ALIGNED TOWARD SHARED GOALS

So what do Dell new hires find when they get to a Dell facility? They find a workforce aligned toward common objectives. And they find individual teams, likewise, aligned toward specific objectives. On the factory floor, people work in teams of two to receive, manufacture, and pack an order for a customer. Profit-sharing programs encourage them to support each other. Metrics are shared on monitors so each team knows how it is doing against factory goals. Mass e-mails are sent to everyone within the organization to recognize outstanding teams. Dell considers ongoing communication critical to his company's success, as important as preventing problems from recurring or brainstorming new product ideas. He wants Dell's people to learn not only about what's happening in senior management but about operations throughout Dell – to learn about "best practices" elsewhere that they can adapt to their own work area.

Dell is a metric-driven company so it is natural that it would use a system like the 360-degree appraisal system. Rather than being evaluated by a single person, their supervisor, employ-ees are evaluated by everyone with whom they work. Dell himself believes that the 360-degree approach both helps iden-tify employee development needs and ensures teams stay focused on their goals. Dell himself practices MBWA – manag-ing by walking around, or "roaming about," as he describes it – observing managers and others at their jobs. Some days he will visit the headquarters building, other days the factory build-ings. He believes that what he experiences better prepares him to make decisions that will impact either Dell's customers or its employees.

Michael Dell's own willingness to continually test new grounds is mirrored in his company's culture. Dell people are taught from the moment they join the organization to ask how work can be done more effectively or efficiently. Dell says, "When you take the historical blinders off, it's amazing what you can accomplish." This kind of thinking works because Dell, unlike many companies, ensures that its employees at all levels know what is happening – corporate plans – and, more important, what needs to be done to achieve those plans. Town hall meetings are held each year at which Dell talks about how the company is achieving its strategies, its current market position, and future plans. Employees have the opportunity to raise questions – and replies, says Dell are honest, not "corporatespeak."

What about "fun"? Can working at Dell be fun, as well as challenging and exciting? Very much so. At Dell, it's as much of the culture as communication, group problem-solving, and teamwork. For instance, several times a year at Dell Computer Corporation's server and storage products plant in Austin, if the plant exceeds its quarterly goals a *management pay up day* event is staged as part of a series of motivational activities. On one occasion, the associates of the plant's morale team had managers take turns getting drenched in a dunking booth as workers enjoyed a *dunk your manager* party. Another time, managers were ordered to put on hula skirts and amuse the workforce.

Think, again, of Charles Handy's reference to fleas and elephants. Dell doesn't recruit elephants. He has programs in place to ensure they don't join his corporate team. Fleas, on the other hand, have the perfect environment to cluster into teams and come up with new and faster ways to grow the business. After all, as Dell observes, his company possesses an open culture in which people feel free to take the most direct route to get the information they need or to come up with and implement a better process or solution. It's very much a part of Dell's competitive edge.

MICHAEL DELL'S PEOPLE-MANAGEMENT FORMULA

Michael Dell has made allies of his employees – and not only because of profit sharing and stock option plans or 401(k) programs that give them stock in Dell rather than straight cash. He's made them allies by:

◆ *Ensuring all hires are winners.* Dell people know they are great by checking out the company they find themselves in – not just Dell Computer Corporation but the talented people with whom they work daily.

◆ *Giving employees the opportunity to make a difference.* Isn't that what talented people want? Dell uses the skills, abilities and knowledge of his people fully – and rewards them accordingly.

◆ *Providing opportunities to learn and grow professionally.* Dell Computer offers the kind of ongoing training that keeps talented people on the top of their field. Working at Dell, they won't stagnate.

◆ *Creating a climate of open communication.* Dell people don't have a chain of command to go through to get the information they want – there isn't one at Dell. They have easy access to the information they need and freedom to test better ways to get their work done or satisfy customer needs.

BIBLIOGRAPHY

"Andy Esparza Knows What Success Sounds Like," *Fast Company,* December 1999.

Dell, Michael and Fredman, Catherine, *Direct from Dell: Strategies That Revolutionized an Industry,* HarperBusiness, New York 1999.

Frieswick, Kris, "Team Teaching," *CFO, The Magazine for Senior Financial Executives,* April 2000.

Harris, Jim and Brannick, Joan, *Finding and Keeping Great Employees,* AMACOM, 1999.

Jacob, Rahul, "The Resurrection of Michael Dell," *Fortune,* September 18, 1995.

Joinson, Carla, "Moving At the Speed of Dell," *HRMagazine,* April 1999.

King, Julia, "Dell Facilitates Recruiting via Video Service," *Computerworld,* September 15, 1997.

"Soggy Managers," *Industry Week,* December 6, 1999.

Whitford, David, "Another Good Day for a Dell Sales Whiz," *Fortune,* July 20, 1998.

Five

BE DIRECT!

Marketing is not a function; it is the whole business seen from the customer's point of view.
– Peter Drucker

W ith his direct approach, Michael Dell took a fledgling company and grew it to the size of the giants in the industry in only a few years. Now he is moving to surpass his firm's chief competitors and block upstart firms that might try to emulate his success by taking his direct-sales model on the Web, reaping all the benefits that this position will provide – from reduced administrative and sales costs to closer customer relationships and insights it offers into market needs, to bottom-line benefits like increased customer retention and loyalty. Dell didn't just make the Web another channel. His observation of the Internet made clear to him that the Internet couldn't be a sideline to core sales projects. "It has to be integrated into your business," Dell has told reporters. And that is exactly what dell.com is. "Now our employees believe they can't make their quotas without the Internet because we set their quotas so high."

GO DIRECT, DELL

Neither move has been easy for Dell. As most people know, his decision to sell direct when he founded his company went against the industry norm. At the time, most computer manufacturers sold through retail channels or resellers. It was a model that Dell in the early years of Dell Computer tested and chose to walk away from. Yes, he could sell computers through retailers but he found when he studied the numbers he couldn't make money that way. The direct model enabled the company to price its products aggressively since it didn't have to deal with the 25 to 45 percent dealer mark-up at the time.

TAKE THE MODEL ABROAD

Despite opposition from analysts, Dell not only stayed with the direct model in the US but also exported it as he went global – first to the UK, then central and western Europe, then China, and now in Brazil, Latin America.

MOVE TO THE WEB

Likewise, Dell reportedly experienced opposition when he decided to sell Dell products on the Internet. In his mind, it was a logical extension, enabling the company to create even stronger relationships with its customers, but members of Dell's management team questioned whether either corporate clients or consumers would buy their computers off the Web. Its sales personnel felt threatened – that they could lose their jobs. But Dell's view was that the Internet would enhance the total customer communication package, as it has done, and enable the company to spend less time selling or giving information over the phone, freeing staff time for customer account management, relationship building, and after-sales service, as have also been so. John Farrell, senior director of channel marketing at Carlson Marketing Group, a Minneapolis-based marketing consulting company, summed it up when he observed that the Internet is actually a tool that can help sales personnel, strengthening their relationship with customers. "It's an opportunity to

> "Knowledge is becoming the only meaningful resource. The traditional factors of production have not disappeared. But they have become secondary."
> – Peter Drucker

communicate more regularly, provide new customer service potential, better handle sales tracking, and deal with price elasticity.

Shikhar Ghosh, chairman of Open Market, Inc., put Internet-based customer service in perspective when he commented that, with the Internet, a company can inexpensively provide a level of personalized service previously offered only by a salesperson. That makes the Internet channel very compelling for customers – and at low cost for the product producer. Certainly, customer response to Dell's online store has been significant.

According to Dell's annual report, the company made $14 million per day by the end of the fourth quarter of fiscal 1999, approximately 25 percent of revenue for that quarter. Dell's goal is to conduct all business online. A study by the Direct Marketing Association found that most successful online marketers were those doing B2B (business-to-business) transactions, particularly in the high-tech area, like Dell with its corporate and institutional customers. The study concluded that e-commerce revenue in the computer and electronics industries would grow to $395.3 billion by 2003, fueled by firms like Dell and Cisco Systems, two big online players. The study noted that 80 percent of Dell's overall business and 60 percent of its online transactions are with other businesses.

MOVE ONE STEP AT A TIME

Dell's initial forays onto the Internet took the form of customer support. As early as the mid-1980s, customers could download software off the Internet rather than wait for the disk to come in the mail. The FTP site became popular and provided a lesson to Dell on the cost savings that the Internet could provide.

WHY COMPANIES AREN'T MARKET-DRIVEN

In his book, *The Market-Driven Organization,* George S. Day uses the phrase "market-driven" to mean customer-focused. That is, market-driven organizations not only understand their markets but they make their customers the final arbiter. Day asks the question, "Why aren't more companies market-driven?" Yes, why aren't there more companies that commit to leadership in the markets they choose to serve and deliver excellence in execution across their enterprise, as well as know their markets and listen to their customers?

In Day's opinion, too many companies are:

◆ *Oblivious to the market.* They are so product-focused that they forget the other part of the equation: the customer. You can produce products but they must be ones that customers want.

◆ *Compelled by the market.* Yes, it is possible to be too market-driven, bending over backwards to satisfy any and all customers, thereby diluting any coordinated effort. This may explain why Dell has segmented its business, to ensure that efforts within different divisions are specifically focused on customer segments.

◆ *Caught in an ego trip.* While some firms blindly follow customers without a clear strategic plan, other firms ignore their customers. Day considers this an especial problem with technology-driven firms. He suggests that their managers think customers never come up with the most valuable innovations. "They fail to see that a market-driven focus can be used to support and inform research and product development without blindly following customers."

◆ *Dominated by short-run cost concerns.* When these thoughts take center stage, an organization becomes unaware of market erosion or diminishing technological advantages. In Dell's case, this is very important right now. As some analysts predict the decline of the PC market, and point out that it means very little to be market leader of a market that is ceasing to exist, Dell already is moving beyond PCs to both the high and low ends of the technology market.

In fact, some customers could even download a patch while they were on the telephone with the Dell technician who could then walk them through installation and configuration of the update. This also let the technician know whether the update would solve the customer's problem. If not, he or she could offer an alternative.

In 1995, Dell launched its site as a means of providing marketing and product support information to the technologically savvy. But quickly the site mushroomed, as its popularity brought potential customers. Consequently, Dell had more product descriptions and technical support information to keep up with customer demand. By fall 1995, Dell installed its first interactive application – a quote generator. This let a customer configure a PC by selecting from groups of options and receive a price quotation. Visitors could add or remove components to see how it affected price. This service brought more potential customers to the site – and also demand by them to be able to order online.

"Dell has great one-to-one relationships with millions of customers around the world. Now it wants to use the Dell brand to sell those customers things other than computers."
– *Forbes*

The message was clear from its customers: Dell needed to create a Web site for customers to configure and order their PC. And Michael Dell and his company have long learned the worth of listening to their customers.

BUILD CUSTOMER LOYALTY

Dell's initial purchasers online were consumers. After all, they already went to the site for product information and price quotes. To get its corporate and institutional clients to purchase online, Dell Computer began an educational program, demonstrating to CIOs how purchasing their computer products online from Dell would simplify the whole thing. Dell set up a variety of Web-based tools to enable clients to track orders and get service support, and even developed password-protected customized Web pages for each corporate client, called Premier Pages, to enable client firms to configure, price, and buy systems at preset prices. The Premier Pages, Dell strongly observes, don't replace line sales reps; rather, they supplement the sales rep's function. When a client firm needs a sales rep, he or she is there. Otherwise, they can handle their transactions directly online.

As Dell has moved his firm online, he has increased the means by which he stays in touch with customers – from Platinum Forums in which he, his management team, and the firm's technicians meet with Dell's largest clients to online and call surveys to smaller client firms and at-home users of Dell computer systems, to systems that link dell.com pages to customer intranets that allow customers to quickly access order and shipping information and place orders and transfer payments to Dell. Dell even has created customer-to-customer relationships using a collaborative public forum over the Web that links customers together to share and solve common technical issues.

USE INFORMATION AS AN ASSET

"The key to using the Internet to extend and build relationships is to view ownership of information differently – you need to bring customers inside your business to create information partnerships. In this way, relationships become the differentiator, more than products or services. Businesses become intertwined, making it extremely difficult for a greenfield competitor to disrupt the intellectual capital surrounding these knowledge-based partnership – unless the competitor comes up with a whole new business system."

– Michael Dell, to a group of businesspeople

WATCH THE COMPETITION

As I write this, Dell Computer's competitors have moved aggressively on Web selling. Compaq's Web site even allows unsure buyers to click a button to send an SOS to Compaq headquarters, prompting an immediate call from a sales rep. Dell doesn't seem as threatened as one would think he should feel. He points to the fact that his competitors have yet to choose to sell either direct or through resellers and, until they do, won't reap the full advantages of the direct model in real time or online, from operational savings to enhancement of the total customer experience. Investors are split on the issue. The downside sees Dell's Internet activity as something that could be easily replicated by any industry competitor willing to sell at lower costs, even if it means big losses at first. The upside sees Dell's active involvement on the Web as possibly the first step into leveraging additional sales and services. They point to Amazon.com, which branched into auctions and pharmaceuticals, even dog food, after its initial entrance as a bookstore. They see the possibility of Dell going into storage products, peripherals and everything else that falls into the corporate computer category. Should Dell expand into these businesses on the Internet, then, say the pundits, Dell's competitors wouldn't have a chance.

While much attention focuses on Dell's direct model and its Web site, less attention has focused on other Dell market innovations, like his decision early in his company's life to provide support services, first via telephone and now online, and also his decision to segment businesses to focus on the specific needs of each of Dell Computer's targeted markets. As Dell himself has mentioned many times, Dell Computer services several markets, from large corporate accounts to small ones, from government agencies (federal and state) to large and smaller educational institutions, to home offices and individual consumers. And, most important, Dell recognized early that knowledge was a critical asset of the new economy, and he has invested in physical assets to gather these intangible assets.

MICHAEL DELL'S TASK LIST FOR YOU

If you want some guidelines to take away with the Dell story, here are six tasks that Michael Dell might suggest:

◆ Recognize that a direct relationship with each of your end customers offers valuable information you can use to better manage business. Further, by going on the Web, you can expand the number of end customers you reach and exponentially increase your knowledge about your markets.

◆ Don't just go on the Internet. Make sure that your Internet activities are fully integrated into your telephone-based sales, order entry, and service functions. Ideally, the relationship between the Internet and other corporate operations should be seamless.

◆ Don't assume that you are limited in the kinds of products you can sell on the Web. As Dell has proven, if you give customers the opportunity to do so, also make it easy for them, and they will purchase relatively expensive products over the Internet.

◆ Don't just sell on your site. Give customers information they need to use your products. If you sell high-tech products, give visitors to your site the same troubleshooting support that your own technical personnel have. You'll save yourself a lot of customer service time and simultaneously give reason for customers to become repeat customers.

◆ If you do B2B, design your site to enable your customers to bring elements of your site into their intranet or otherwise link to integrate your processes with their own. Think about something like Dell's Premier Pages for its customers. Now Dell even links with customers' accounting systems to facilitate purchasing. You'll keep customers longer and extend your company's reach within customer organizations.

◆ Don't let the Web replace personal communication with your customers – large accounts or small. In particular, when it comes to large accounts, you want to build direct relationships with customers' employees. After all, they really are your customers.

DON'T SIT ON YOUR LAURELS

Some analysts say that Dell may be market leader in PC sales, but that there is little to be said about being leader in a dying market. "The party is over," says Fred A. Hickey, editor of the newsletter *High-Tech Strategist*. PCs have become a commodity just like televisions. But Dell is optimistic about the future. "Change is not something we've ever shied away from," he has said. He plans to move Dell into other product areas, such as high-end servers and services. Dell told a group of executives that the Internet is moving computer companies in two directions: toward high-priced servers and huge storage systems and lower-cost cell phones and handheld devices, as well as PCs. His company's plan is to produce products for both markets. His firm will also move into Web hosting and storage, new revenue streams. Dell noted that server industry sales will grow twentyfold, but the market currently belongs primarily to Sun Microsystems with its Unix systems and a $1.4 billion annual research budget (five times that of Dell). Dell executives say the battle will be waged in the price arena. Referring to Sun Microsystems, Tom Meredith observed, "They have had no competition for the past few years. If I were them, I'd take a razor to my operating expenses right now." Analysts say that Dell will take on Sun with the same plan he used with Compaq, IBM, and Hewlett-Packard: sell direct, win on price, keep customer loyalty with quality.

HOW HAS HE DONE SO FAR?

In early 1999, Dell formed a team called Dell Technical Consultants that trains customers on how to maintain and integrate

Dell products such as servers and network-attached storage appliances into their organizations.

In the same year, Dell formed Dell Ventures, an investment arm. So far it has put $70 million into around 90 companies not only to make money but also to use the partnerships to fuel Dell's continuing growth. For instance, in 1999, the company purchased ConvergeNet Technologies Inc., its first acquisition. The first product from the acquisition, called the Storage Domain Manager, will sit between servers and the storage area network, enabling IT administrators to manage, switch, route, and partition data without overburdening the servers. Besides the Storage Domain Manager, the new acquisition's team will work on upgrades and additions to Dell's Fiber Channel Power-Vault product line. "The challenge for Dell will be in managing a development environment," says Robert Gray, an analyst for International Data Corporation. "You can't schedule invention. And Dell is a company that manages its technical suppliers with a delivery in 20 minutes or less."

> "Everyone had a phone, many sat next to one all day long in their offices. It could provide immediate connection not just for selling but to handle queries, provide after-sales support, and 'keep the customers satisfied.' "
> – **Michael De Kare-Silver (quoting Dell defending the direct model),** *E-Shock*

Last year, Dell also launched a group called Gigabuys to resell software, Epson printers, Kodak digital cameras, and 3Com palms. In early 2000, it formed Office by Dell to sell office equipment, from chalkboards to leather chairs.

Then, in spring 2000, Dell Computer announced it would broaden its Dell Ventures activities to include equity investments and incubation services for early-stage private companies. According to Michael Dell, the firm will go beyond investment in start-ups to include assistance with strategy development and access to professional services. "We are particularly interested in early-stage companies with products and services which have the potential to create breakthroughs in the evolving Internet age, with an aim to integrate those products and services into Dell's business and drive our future growth."

> "On the face of it, Dell is a hyper-efficient distributor. Beneath, it's something else. Dell aggregates knowledge and turns it into a control point."
> **– Adrian Slywotszky (author of *Profit Patterns*), Fortune**

At the same time, Dell Computer announced its plan to create a new Web site for smaller business, called www.DellEWorks.com, that would give customers a "one-stop source to establish an Internet presence and grow their businesses with online services such as direct mail, direct e-mail, public relations, recruiting, credit reports, training and market research." "Dell has the experience and expertise to be an outstanding provider of products and services to build an Internet business," said Frank Muehleman, vice-president and general manager of Dell's home and small business group." According to *Business Wire*, only 26 percent of smaller businesses have a Web site, and only 15 percent have a Web storefront. So www.DellEWorks.com is designed to help firms to achieve both of these.

What else is Dell up to? The firm teamed with *Government Technology* magazine and Microsoft to create a dynamic Web portal for the exchange of information in the growing electronic government field.

Dell would seem to have many coals in the fire – and with cause. After all, every so many months, Dell executives get an unusual assignment: play the part of a competitor and devise a plan for destroying Dell. The result is not only defensive plans but offensive plans for the future.

BIBLIOGRAPHY

Callahan, Sean, "DMA Study: Marketers Making Money Online: High-Tech Companies Lead the Way in Showing Internet Helps Bottom Line," *Business Marketing*, May 1, 1999.

Cohan, Peter S., *E-Profit: High Payoff Strategies for Capturing the E-Commerce Edge*, AMACOM, New York 2000.

Day, George S., *The Market-Driven Organization: Understanding, Attracting and Keeping Valuable Customers*, The Free Press, New York 1999.

De Kare-Silver, Michael, *E-Shock: The Electronic Shopping Revolution: Strategies for Retailers and Manufacturers*, AMACOM, New York 1999.

Dell, Michael and Fredman, Catherine, *Direct from Dell: Strategies That Revolutionized an Industry*, HarperBusiness, New York 1999.

"Dell Ventures Activity Expanded to Include Incubation," Dell press release, March 29, 2000.

DiCarlo, Lisa, "Dell Forges New Ventures to Expand Business," *PC Week*, June 28, 1999.

DiCarlo, Lisa, "New Dell Initiatives Leverage Net," *PC Week*, August 30, 1999.

"Didn't Delliver," *The Economist* (UK), February 20, 1999.

"Dynamic Duo," *Business Wire*, April 4, 2000.

Horowitz, Alan S., "The Cisco Sales Machine," *Selling Power*, May 2000.

Lelii, Sonia R., "Dell Shifts SAN Strategy with First Acquisition," *PC Week*, September 13, 1999.

Lyons, Daniel, "Michael Dell's Second Act," *Forbes*, April 17, 2000.

Lundquist, Eric, "Dell's Web Tie-In Could Unravel Compaq," *PC Week*, May 17, 1999.

"New Dell Internet Site Helps Small Businesses Start and Run Their Companies over the Web," *Business Wire*, April 5, 2000.

"Selling Secrets of a PC Tycoon," *Computer Weekly*, February 11, 1999.

Seybold, Patricia B., *Customers.Com: How to Create a Profitable Business Strategy for the Internet and Beyond*, Times Business, Random House, New York 1998.

Slywotsky, Adrian J., "Taking the Low Road," *Sales & Marketing Management*, January 1996.

Stepanek, Marcia, "What Does No. 1 Do for an Encore?' *Business Week*, November 2, 1998.

Stewart, Thomas A., "Grab the Knowledge and Squeeze: GET A GRIP," *Fortune*, November 8, 1999.

Six

YOU ARE YOUR CUSTOMERS

Our goal as a company is to have customer service that is not just the best but legendary.
– Sam Walton (Founder of Wal-Mart)

Michael Dell isn't that interested in the technology nor is he focused on his competitors, although like any good businessman he monitors their actions. What interests Michael Dell is his customers, present and future, and the quality of service and satisfaction his organization offers. The products his company sells are important to Dell but only to be sure that they are what Dell customers want. When it comes to firms like Compaq, Hewlett-Packard and Gateway, his interest is in how Dell can surpass them in price, product, and performance in service, from delivery time to support.

DELL'S MISSION STATEMENT

The importance to Michael Dell of the total customer experience is evident in the mission statement for his company on its Web site. It reads:

Dell's mission is to be the most successful computer company in the world at delivering the best customer experience in markets we serve. In doing so, Dell will meet customer expectations of:

◆ highest quality;

◆ leading technology;

◆ competitive pricing;

◆ individual and company accountability;

◆ best in class service and support;

◆ flexible customization capability;

◆ superior corporate citizenship; and

◆ financial stability.

Except for the last two items, all relate to the customer experience with Dell, from the moment he or she chooses to consider a Dell product to the moment it is discarded and replaced by another Dell model. Dell considers the first six elements critical to the total customer experience, the basis for competitive advantage in the future. It is certainly critical to Dell's differentiating from its competitors.

Dell had consumers in mind when he originally conceived of letting them order IBM PCs with the special features they wanted. Now his company appeals to businesses because it can so easily preconfigure each computer to their precise requirements, something other computer companies are finding hard to do. For a large oil company, for instance, Dell preloads its machines with proprietary software that tracks sales at the company's gas stations across the country. Dell even pastes inventory tags on each computer so that they can be delivered promptly to the right end-user's desk. Consumers and corporate and institutional clients alike can get this kind of quality service, whether online or via more traditional fax or phone, as part of Dell's effort to "delight customers."

HOW TO DELIGHT YOUR CUSTOMERS

If you were to ask Michael Dell how your organization should go about delighting its customers he might come up with these guidelines:

◆ *Find ways to talk to your customers.* Dell's direct model does it naturally, but it is supplemented with the Platinum Council for larger accounts, online and phone surveys for smaller businesses and consumers.

◆ *Don't just talk to your customers; listen to them.* Dell himself fell short of this once – in 1994, when his firm proceeded with a product line despite little interest from customers. That one experience – a serious shortfall in the company's otherwise exceptional history – has left a lasting impression on Dell – and has since been reflected both in procedures and culture.

◆ *Create opportunities for shared savings.* As you listen, determine the kinds of problems they are encountering and how you can address them to the mutual advantage of your customers and you.

◆ *Make communication as important to your customers as it is to you.* You need to learn from them their requirements, expectations, and wants. But they want to learn from you about your plans for the future as they make their own purchasing plans.

◆ *Segment the market.* This way you are better able to satisfy the specific needs of each group of customers. From a management perspective, it also makes it easier to monitor ROIC (return on invested capital), a critical measurement at Dell.

◆ *Use the Internet to provide added value to your customers.* Don't look at the Internet as another channel but rather integrate it into the organization. Think outside the box to find ways to use it to improve service delivery and support.

CREATING A CUSTOMER-FOCUSED CULTURE

Dell told a reporter early in his company's history how important he regarded a customer-focused culture. "At Dell, we are intent on customer satisfaction, so we empower our employees to make fixes and do special things for customers. Having a group of passionate employees who understand the company's agenda and are energized about helping customers is a huge competitive advantage."

Is superior service as important to those who buy online as those who call in their orders? According to Dell, it may be even more important. In a presentation to a business group in August 1999, Michael Dell said that e-shoppers "are more loyal to a customer experience than traditional drivers like product or price." He said that the two factors that seemed to drive e-loyalty were quality of customer service and online delivery. Consequently, Dell's goal was to tie a superior online experience to a superior physical one (that is, delivery and service support) while creating the world's largest NT-commerce site to increase the level of convenience to corporate and institutional accounts, about 90 percent of Dell business. Of this group, at least 70 percent are large enough customers that they buy at least $1 million in PCs annually.

DELL.COM

Since Dell wants eventually to move 100 percent of its business online, online service is extremely important.

For this audience, Dell has created its Premier Page strategy. The company has more than 27,000 Premier Pages or Web pages that allow its customers to access automated paperless purchase orders, custom-defined configurations, order tracking and status, and customized service tools. There is a special Web site for each and every customer that reflects all parts of the relationship – from account contacts to the special prices they get to the nondisclosure of future product information, to a quarterly review that we have with them to make sure that we're meeting their performance requirements, to the technical support information and, of course, commerce. Some customers have on their Premier Page purchase history data so they can see where the product was shipped, who bought it, and the nature of the product.

"Our customer strategy is one area where our model has evolved. We've become good at developing what we call 'scalable' businesses – that is, those in which we can grow revenues faster than expenses. We really look closely at financial measures like gross margins by customer segment – and we focus on segments we can serve profitably as we achieve scale."
– Michael Dell

On the tech-support side, each time Dell builds a PC, it identifies it with a five-digit alphanumeric code. A customer can use that code to get support help. The site will test the system for year 2000 compliance; if it isn't compliant, the customer can download suitable software that will make it so. There are self-diagnostic tools for troubleshooting. It even provides access to help desks for the same tools that Dell's internal technical-support reps use. "This doesn't result in major cost savings for Dell," Dell told a group of business people in May 1999. "But it *has* resulted in significant cost-savings for our customers, enriching their relationships with Dell."

For smaller businesses Dell will create one of these pages as well, Michael Dell told an audience of executives, "When Biggo Tires in Cleveland calls us ad says, 'We want a Premier Page too, because we're going to buy 50 computers a year,' we can set one of these up for them in a few minutes." In the future, according to Dell, his company's systems will link directly to customers' existing procurement systems. If Dell can practice what it has labeled "direct commerce integration," it could save customers both time and money because the data wouldn't have to be entered more than once, then passed through their procurement operations. Dell said, "The goal is to deepen customer relationships by providing added convenience, cost savings, and efficiency for them, and a wider array of services."

CUSTOMER SAVINGS

According to Dell, response to the Premier Pages has been excellent. One customer told him it had saved $10 million a year in productivity improvements, now that it can track information-technology assets and get improved technical support. Another said it had saved $4 million through procurement costs alone. "When we sign up new customers, we're now essentially saying in our interaction with them, 'Let's engage together on the Internet.' And they seem excited not only by that but by the results."

While Dell is most thought of as a supplier to giant companies, as is evident from the above, it isn't interested only in big companies and institutions. "If you go back to 1994, our US business had a group of large customers. It was a $3.5 billion business," Dell told a group of businesspeople in Georgia in summer 1999. In recent years, the business has segmented customers by size and buying criteria. Besides medium and large and giant companies and government and educational institutions, the company also services smaller businesses and, most recently, it launched a campaign directed at consumers for Web-PCs.

SEGMENTING BUSINESSES

Among smaller businesses, Dell Computer Corporation is number one among PC makers, up from fourth place three years before. Dell's sales to home and small business customers grew 70 percent from 1998 to 1999. In 1999, it made up 30 percent of revenues, i.e. around $8 billion. This has come about because Dell goes out of the way to make its small-business companies feel as important as it does its large accounts.

It is the responsibility of Dell reps to get to truly know the heads of the smaller companies that make up their territory – to the point that an account manager might be thought of as "an adopted sister" by CEO of one of her corporate clients. Dell has a team of around 150 "relationship sales reps" that services its thousands of small-business customers. These companies include brick-and-mortar firms, as well as dot.coms. Kevin Rollins, Dell vice-chairman, told a member of the press, "We love the dot-coms. They've got 85 employees and 400 servers. They're going to be great customers for us."

Although industry trends suggest that these smaller businesses (defined by Dell as any company with fewer than 400 employees) tend to change from one PC supplier to another due to price, about two thirds of Dell's small-business clients represent repeat business. This success is attributable not only to lower costs, due to Dell's direct model, but also to how Dell "touches" these customers and builds a relationship with them. All a smaller customer has to put down is $40,000 a year with Dell, and it gets a dedicated account rep. Since most reps manage only around 70 clients each, they can give these smaller businesses comparable attention to that given to the corporate giants. There are also services that come with Dell – like the customized Premier Page that lets these smaller businesses place orders on the Web, track what they've bought, and access the Dell Plus program which means company technicians pre-load their computers with any software they want, including proprietary software of their own.

"The total customer experience – including an emphasis on service and speed – is the next competitive frontier."
– **Michael Dell,**
Direct from Dell.

"The idea is to let a small company with 100 employees have the same end-to-end relationship with us as a large corporation," Dell account manager, Jacqueline Godlewski, told Daniel Lyons of *Forbes.*

People like Godlewski have been trained not only to respond quickly to their customers' needs but also to be proactive with customers. Godlewski told Lyons how one of her clients rented space in a computer outsourcing facility that charged customers according to the amount of rack space. When Dell's engineers started developing a new, smaller server, she called her client to tell him about the model since it could save him money because it took up less rack space.

THE FOUNDATION FOR A CUSTOMER SATISFACTION PROGRAM

Even before you can provide the kind of customer service that Dell offers, you need a solid customer-satisfaction program. Here are ten elements that are essential to such an initial step. Each one must be followed, or the foundation essential to delighting customers will crumble. These rules come from Earl Naumann's book *Creating Customer Value: The Path to Sustainable Competitive Advantage.*

1. *Involve top management.* What does Naumann mean by that? Top management shouldn't think it can get away with a few public talks or memos on the subject. Only when top management gathers customer satisfaction data, sits in on cross-functional team meetings, and asks, "What is being done here to improve the situation?" will the importance of customer satisfaction become apparent.

2. *Know your customers.* There are lots of companies that know about their markets in general but know very little about their customers specifically, and that is what makes the difference between a market-driven and customer-driven firm. Customer-driven organizations view each customer segment as a valuable asset and work to increase their asset base by learning what is important to each.

3. *Let customers tell you what is important to them.* Survey your customers to find out. Not only must you discover what your customers want but you must learn in "customers' own words"; as Naumann observed, "If those wants are quickly translated into the language of the firm, such as 'technical specifications,' something may be lost in the transaction."

4. *Know your customers' requirements, expectations, and wants.* Naumann believes customer information should be categorized into these three groups. Requirements are those attributes that customers must have. Expectations are product or service standards that customers should be able to expect. Wants are those things that customers would like to have but don't really expect. Dell would probably consider these as the basis for "customer delight."

5. *Know the criteria that influence customers' decisions.* Don't just know each attribute but its relative importance. During research, customers can be asked to describe a critical situation when they were either very satisfied or dissatisfied. Sifting through these memories should determine a pattern that yields customer satisfaction.

6. *Gather and trust the data.* If you have done some focus groups or other meetings, you have some sense of the attributes that are important to customers. Now you need to develop a questionnaire to get harder data that measures the customers' perceptions of the firm's ability to deliver each attribute, the importance of each attribute, and your firm's performance against that of competitors.

7. *Benchmark against competitors.* You want to do an industry-wide comparison and then you want to benchmark against key competitors.

8. *Develop cross-functional action plans.* As Naumann observed, "The real litmus test of research is that it provides direction for organizational change and improvement." Based on studies of both hard and soft issues, your firm should make internal changes to increase customer satisfaction. When the results of such investigation don't lead to changes within the organization, then the entire effort has been useless.

9. *Measure continually and spread the data.* You won't see 100 percent improvement overnight. But by striving to reach that goal, you will see continual improvements.

10. *Commit to getting better and better and better.* Never assume you can't improve further. Over time, every program can be enhanced. But if you do it right the first time, subsequent improvements need only be minor.

In late 1999, Dell unleashed its biggest mass consumer marketing effort around a Web-centric PC that its marketing announcements say makes Web surfing easier and more fun. The new model is targeted at all consumers, from the youngest to oldest in the family. Commenting on the development, Van Baker, an analyst with Dataquest, suggested: "Dell is trying to establish a brand that begins to talk to consumers, and they're trying to get people to pick up the phone and call them or go to the Web. They firmly believe that once they get the attention of consumers, they'll get them and retain them." Certainly, Dell isn't the first of the leading computer companies to address this market. Actually, Dell is never first in anything, as Tim Bajarin, president of Creative Strategies Research International, a high-tech consulting firm, observes. "Dell's style is to let other guys do the evangelism and, then, at the right point come into the market with a superior product, marketing, and distribution. Michael Dell doesn't haphazardly just go into a market."

Van Baker believes Dell expects that about five to ten percent of consumer sales will be of its WebPC, with replacement purchases driving sales opportunity. Van Baker considers its release an attempt to get beyond the traditional Dell customer base and establish Dell as a consumer PC product company.

In an article in *Fortune*, reporter Eryn Brown suggested that Dell could be the very best PC maker. She observed that Dell isn't colorful; the products it produces don't represent "fabulous new technology." She also pointed to the fact that Dell doesn't have a cult following (say, like Amazon.com). Michael Dell himself is a solid businessman, but his personality has been described as "plain vanilla." Yet, she said, Dell is one of the most savvy and emulated companies in the business. Why? What separates it from the pack of high-tech firms is its ability to do exactly what its competitors believe cannot be done – from its direct model to its export of that model abroad to its successful sale of PCs over the Web.

CUSTOMER FEEDBACK

What Brown fails to mention is just how the direct model and online sales facilitate feedback that lets the company respond immediately to shifting demand and keeps the company from being stuck with PCs nobody wants. By gathering this vast amount of data, Dell can plot both its short- and long-term strategic path. Dell reportedly has over 25,000 specially trained employees who take comments from customers and organize these comments. According to Sharon Voros, author of *The Road to CEO*, Dell believes it is essential that literally everyone hears the voice of the customer, including the frustrations when the firm does something that makes it hard for a customer to use a Dell product.

As Dell himself points out, "When you engage directly with your customers, you begin to develop an intimate understanding of their likes, needs, and priorities." They want to tell you what works for them and what doesn't and why. In the process,

THE ISSUE OF ASSETS IN THE NEW ECONOMY

In their book *Cracking the Value Code: How Successful Businesses Are Creating Wealth in the New Economy,* authors Richard E.S. Boulton, Barry D. Libert and Steve M. Samek point to the increasing importance of intangible assets for competitive advantage. The authors, all partners at Arthur Andersen, surveyed 10,000 companies to determine what represents value in the new millennium. Results showed that intangible assets included a company's leaders, its employees, its supplier relationships (think about virtual integration used by Dell to speed delivery and reduce operating costs) and, relevant to this chapter, its customers.

The authors suggest readers ask themselves five questions. Within the context of Dell's efforts to "delight" customers, ask yourself:

◆ Do we effectively manage our customers to create value?
◆ Have we created a mix of customers, channels, and affiliates (think suppliers) that increase customer value?
◆ Can our company adapt any aspect of Dell's online efforts to our own management of customer assets to make them more effective?
◆ Are we tracking the quality of our service and measuring our performance? Are we also tracking the value-creating contributions of our customers to our sales?
◆ Are our competitors gaining advantage with their customer assets that we aren't? If so, why? Are we missing out on an opportunity?

you can identify new ideas for products and services, ideas that, as Dell himself has acknowledged, are worth millions of R&D dollars. Indeed, this ongoing communication with its customers may be one reason why Dell can operate with what is a relatively lean R&D function. His firm's customers not only identify refinements for Dell products but suggest new products and services for study. He regards this as a direct result of his decision, since he founded the company, to build systems to order. Customer feedback doesn't come solely during transactions. Information from its largest customers also comes from face-to-face meetings, including its Platinum Councils where customers – corporate and now universities – meet Dell senior technologists to focus on customers' changing needs and product plans for the future.

Smaller customers and consumers respond to online surveys and real-time focus groups. The company also uses outbound call surveys that solicit feedback. By gathering information from each and every customer, Dell not only knows what they want to buy and deliver but also their needs for the future. Dell has told reporters that customers also gain from the exchange. In return for the information they give about their requirements for products and services, they in turn learn about new products and industry trends that help them make decisions about their own computer systems – whether major account or home computer owner.

CUSTOMIZING COMMUNICATION FOR CUSTOMERS

Bob Langer, director of dell.com, believes that it is imperative that Dell offers customers multiple ways of getting the information and service they need. He pointed to four ways that Dell does this in an article in *Association Management:*

◆ *Customer to system.* Since Dell tags the products it builds, when customers call or go online, all they need do is provide their service tag number. Dell then can respond with the most accurate and relevant information in answer to their queries.

◆ *Customer to knowledge base.* Dell has a search engine whereby users can enter in plain English a request to locate specific information. That includes the status of their orders online.

◆ *Customer to customer.* Yes, customers can engage in online chats with customers with similar product configurations, needs, and interests.

◆ *Customer to Dell.* Yes, behind dell.com there are real people who can handle problems by e-mail or, yes, even phone for those people who still prefer interacting directly with a Dell employee. That's unlikely to change even as Dell moves more and more online. "Direct is Dell," said Langer. "Without the direct model – without the direct contact with customers – Dell would not be Dell."

Dell was only a fledgling company when Michael Dell wrote an article for *Planning Review.* In that article, he likened service to a product that Dell sold. That is still true to this day. Among its assets, Dell Computer can measure the customer loyalty built on its customer responsiveness.

BIBLIOGRAPHY

Brown, Eryn, "Could the Very Best PC Maker be Dell Computer?" *Fortune,* April 14, 1997.

Boulton, Richard E.S., Libert, Barry D. and Samek, Steve M., *Cracking the Value Code: How Successful Businesses Are Creating Wealth in the New Economy*, HarperBusiness, 2000.

"Dell Gets Wired," *Computer Weekly,* May 7, 1998.

Dell, Michael and Fredman, Catherine, *Direct from Dell: Strategies That Revolutionized an Industry*, HarperBusiness, New York 1999.

Dell, Michael, "Making the Right Choices for the New Consumer," *Planning Review*, September–October 1993.

Elkin, Tobi, "Dell Ads Aim at Broad Target," *Advertising Age,* December 6, 1999.

Espe, Erik, "Hardware Wars," *The Business Journal,* December 24, 1999.

Hignite, Karla B., "Customizing to the Max," *Association Management,* August 1999.

Lyons, Daniel, "Make the Little Guys Feel Big," *Forbes,* April 17, 2000.

Naumann, Earl, *Creating Customer Value: The Path to Sustainable Competitive Advantage*, Thomas Executive Press 1995.

Voros, Sharon, *The Road to CEO*, Adams Media Corporation, Holbrook, MA 2000.

Seven

NEVER STOP IMPROVING

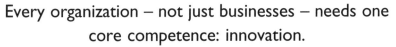

Every organization – not just businesses – needs one core competence: innovation.
– Peter Drucker, "The Information Executives Truly Need," *Harvard Business Review*

D ell Computer Corporation practices "innovative thinking." More important, however, Dell and its CEO "teach innovative thinking," observes Michael Dell in his book *Direct from Dell.*

It should go without saying that one of the largest computer companies in the world would encourage innovative thinking. Indeed, it would seem ridiculous for any enterprise today not to do so. In an editorial in the *Harvard Business Review,* the then editor Theodore Levitt wrote, "Change is the order of the day ... Choose it or die." Such an exhortation would seem a waste of print space, yet almost nine years later there are still organizations that do not encourage innovation either in the products they make or the processes by which they produce them. True, as Michael Dell has said, "There's no risk in preserving the status quo." But, as he adds, "There's no profit, either!"

UNDERSTAND THE NEED FOR INNOVATION

Consider the many strategic challenges organizations face now and will continue to do so in this first decade of the new millennium. These are some reasons why companies must always be open to new ideas:

◆ *An increasing rate of change.* Changes aren't only occurring rapidly, but the significance of these changes is also growing.

◆ *Increasing levels of competition*. In some industries, the competition will be over market share (e.g., steel industry). In others, like consumer products, the opportunities will lie in the creation of new offerings. In the high-tech arena, no question, the race will be won by the swiftest – i.e. the firm able to stay ahead of the technology curve. Actually, the race in each industry will go to the firm that is able to give customers exactly what they want as soon as they realize they need it and, further, find a way for customers to easily get what they want. In Dell's case, its decision to take marketing to the Web reflects the latter.

◆ *The globalization of business competition*. As Professors Fred Luthans, John W. Slocum Jr and Richard Hodgetts wrote in the Autumn 1999 issue of *Organization Dynamics*, "The major multinationals are big and getting bigger. This is going to present a major challenge for executives in both small and large organizations that want to penetrate the overseas markets in which they are supreme in the years ahead."

◆ *Rapid technological change*. In the high-tech arena, this is very much a part of doing business. One tech firm would seem to develop a new technology only to have a competitor produce something faster or more sophisticated, gaining the competitive advantage until another firm leapfrogs over with new technology of its own. An example is Seagate Technology. Until it introduced its 5.25-inch disk drive, the standard was eight-inch drives, but Seagate Technology saw an emerging market in desktop PCs. This story has since repeated itself as new upstart firms introduced 3.5-inch drives and supplanted the 5.25-inch manufacturers.

Even organizations that don't manufacture high-tech products but need them to produce their products will be confronted with the strategic implications of technological developments. The organization that installs the newest technology has a strategic advantage over its competitors until they adopt similar technology.

◆ *A shift in worker values.* For some time now, we have seen evidence of the change in expectations of employees as they seek more meaningful work. This includes a desire to make a difference, which translates into the opportunity to practice "out-of-the-box" thinking.

◆ *The shift from an industrial to a knowledge-based society.* It is ironic that at a time when so many companies have begun to recognize the worth of their intellectual capital, they are losing it through restructuring and other corporate initiatives that lead to staff cuts of their most experienced employees. Still, there is no question of how critical knowledge is – whether it is the old-fashioned experience or information about customers and suppliers – or how it will become more important. Luthans, Slocum, and Hodgetts cite a corporate example that demonstrates the worth of information. Chrysler was traditionally third member of the "big three" US automakers until the mid-eighties when it decided to manufacture minivans. Customer research indicated a desire for these vehicles, a need that competitors' research failed to discern. As a result, Chrysler wound up ahead of the other automakers, which led subsequently to creation of DaimlerChrysler.

Luthans, Slocum, and Hodgetts attribute the Chrysler story, and others like it, not solely to the need to remain at the cutting edge but also to changing market demands – which require awareness of ever-shifting customer demands. "Each of the firms that was eventually displaced had been successful in its own right and was carefully focused on its own customer base. The problem was that the customer was pleased with what the company was currently providing," say Luthans, Slocum, and Hodgetts. Consequently, the firms weren't motivated to ask questions for the purpose of learning about emerging needs. Their managements were unwilling to forgo a currently profitable product for one that offered *potentially* greater promise. "These firms were blinded by both their customers' current needs and management's low tolerance to 'thinking-out-of-the-box.'"

"Change is the order of the day ... Choose it or die."
– Theodore Levitt

While this book is about Dell, a technology firm, the need to "practice innovative thinking" clearly isn't limited to the computer industry. In researching an earlier book on Amazon.com, I studied extensively Wal-Mart, which began expanding its operations in the 1970s. The company offered products that were lower-priced and not very appealing to those who shopped at Sears and J.C. Penney. However, as Wal-Mart's quality improved and its prices declined, it stole customers from these competitors. Customers rejected Sears and J.C. Penney because they no longer satisfied their needs and they took their money to Wal-Mart where they felt they could get more value. Wal-Mart's strategy has been so successful that today its sales are greater than Sears and J.C. Penney combined.

DEVELOP AN ENTREPRENEURIAL ATTITUDE

In writing about the need to "practice innovative thinking," it might seem that we are talking solely to and about entrepre-

neurial firms. Not so. Certainly Dell is no longer an entrepreneurial firm in terms of size, but the actions it takes and other
innovative mega-enterprises – 3M, Bell Labs, and the like –
are entrepreneurial in nature and can significantly impact the
marketplace of the new millennium.

Like many major corporations, Dell uses product teams to make
market breakthroughs. These groups and others like them can
emulate the spirt of entrepreneurship in upstarts. To be truly
entrepreneurial, members of these groups are willing to make
mistakes in order to learn – a position that Dell supports. Admit mistakes, he has written, and move on. The purpose isn't
to please top management – which is too true of bureaucratic
enterprises – but rather to please customers and themselves.
Jean Lipman-Blumen and Harold J. Leavitt, also writing in
Organizational Dynamics, use the term "hot groups" to describe
the kind of product teams and other venture groups that large
organizations need to ensure speed, flexibility, and creativity.
Bill Gates' description of a programming group he belonged
to before the birth of Microsoft is, according to Lipman-Blumen
and Leavitt, typical of a hot group, one willing to come in 24
hours a day straight to create great things fast. They aren't
exclusive to the tech area, either, although there are extensive
examples in that area, like John Sculley's description of the
Macintosh design group at young Apple Computer. But 3M
and the old Bell Laboratories have nurtured hot groups within
them. Hot groups can prosper in organizations whose culture
values the search for information – like Dell – and whose management accepts the fact that today's products may have little
value in tomorrow's markets, and consequently they must always be engaged in learning what their customers value, even
if the signs are only small blips on the market radar.

MEETINGS FOR CREATIVE PROBLEM SOLVING

When meeting rooms were caves, the cave dwellers enjoyed the creativity that came from sitting as a group, coming up with ways to bring down a giant mammoth or another animal for dinner before another cave found a way. Today, meetings are held in brick-and-mortar buildings or on screens linked electronically, but the intention of the groups is often the same: to come up with the means to compete successfully. At a firm like Dell Computer, the means might be a new product, or an improvement in an existing offering, or manufacture of a product, or management of some part of the organization.

In their book *When Sparks Fly: Igniting Creativity in Groups,* authors Dorothy Leonard and Walter Swap describe a five-step process for group creativity, pointing to the benefits of a group process for innovative thinking.

1. *Preparation.* An important step in that preparation is the selection of individuals with track records for out-of-box thinking. But even before this is the decision to use teams for innovation. Leonard and Swap write: "Groups have a potential advantage over an individual because multiple reservoirs of deep expertise can be tapped." They add that two heads or more are better than one, provided three conditions are met:

   ◆ those in the group have useful knowledge;
   ◆ they are capable of accessing that information; and
   ◆ all that information can be shared and synthesized by the group in addressing the innovation opportunity.

2. *Innovation opportunity.* At Dell, questions are often used to stimulate thinking that in turn leads to opportunities for innovation.
   The opportunity might be for improvement in either a technology
   or business approach, or might be a way to overcome a threat or
   shortcoming against a competitor. Leonard and Swap add that one
   innovation often stimulates critical thinking that leads to another
   idea. They point to Xerox whose technological invention of the
   copier machine required a marketing innovation to work. It was
   already possible to make single copies with carbon paper; it took
   recognition of the worth of multiple copies of the same quality to
   make the technological advance worthwhile.

3. *Generating options.* Within this step, there are other steps, as those
   familiar with the problem-solving process are aware. It's very easy
   to grasp the very first idea and go with it without further consideration. Group creativity allows many ideas to come from the
   team, from which the best among the good ones can be chosen.
   Further, any effort at creative thinking must be preceded by a
   clear understanding of the problem being solved or opportunity
   being pursued. Poorly defined problems often recur; likewise,
   opportunities that are not well researched aren't tapped as well
   as they could be.

4. *Incubation.* Many creative groups stall, unable to identify a work-
   able solution to a problem that hasn't been tried, or to develop
   a realistic action plan for pursuing an opportunity. Calling time
   out allows the unconscious work on the problem while the con-
   scious mind addresses work routine. Generally, when the group
   re-assembles, the subconscious has done its work, and the group
   can move to the next, and sometimes most difficult, stage of the
   process.

5. *Selecting an action plan.* The more good ideas that the group generates, the more difficult this process can be. The team leader may act as coach and, sometimes, referee. Say Leonard and Swap, "The same people whose 'off-the-wall' approach benefits the group or organization during creation of options can be a pain in the collective neck when the time comes to agree on action." Beyond that, the chosen alternative may stimulate further options – or midcourse, or even end assessment may demand further brainstorming. A group may also fail to clear a hurdle related to resources available and consequently have to return to divergent thinking or rethink their solution to overcome the objections. Management evaluations would increase what Michael Dell would likely call "smart experimentation" and consequently is not antithetical to creativity – only a part of doing good business.

AVOID THE ICARUS SYNDROME

Remember the Greek myth about the proud lad who wished to fly like the birds and created wax wings to emulate them? His success so clouded his mind that he flew too close to the sun. His artificial wax wings melted and he plunged to his death in the Aegean Sea. In the context of businesses, financial success can seduce companies to accept the status quo and complacency. In his book Dell likens it to managing in a rearview mirror. "In this economy," he says, "you can bet you will end up smashing right into the future. Just to stay competitive, you have to constantly question everything you do."

As Dell observes, and the Icarus myth demonstrates, pride can create a false sense of security. There is the potential danger of believing that one success will beget another success and that this in turn will generate another success. A company can be blinded to trends and opportunities literally before them. "They can stop trying to find ever better new ways of doing things and may become oblivious to emerging trends." To demonstrate his point, Dell cites Digital Equipment whose CEO, Ken Olsen, was featured in 1986 on the cover of *Fortune* with the caption "America's most successful entrepreneur." But a cover shot on *Fortune* means little as history proved – Digital was eventually acquired by Dell's chief competitor Compaq, but shares at that point were one-quarter the rate of those at its apex, due according to Dell, to its failure to move from a centralized proprietary computing model to a model based on industry standards.

UNDERSTAND THE FOUNDATION OF INNOVATION

As you'll discover in Chapter 8, Dell Computer Corporation has made its employees feel and, more important, act like owners. One way that this is played out is in the questions they ask of themselves, co-workers, customers, suppliers, and the like. Asking questions is a part of a learning process, important to Dell who sees openness to new ideas critical to his and employees' ability to utilize their full potential. "Let's face it: if we took all the knowledge we had gleaned from 1993 and 1994 and said, 'That's all we need to know,' I probably wouldn't be writing this book," says Dell in *Direct from Dell*. "But since the start of our company, we have had to learn at a voracious pace just to keep up. That's no small feat, given how quickly our jobs change." But asking questions also leads to new ideas, and new ideas can lead to competitive advantage. "Study the obvious for non-obvious solutions." Dell tells his employees to go to customers and ask them various questions, both technological and service questions. From such dialogues will come innovative thinking. "Constantly question – even the good stuff. There's no better way to improve."

In his book Dell shares an example of how innovative thinking achieved a competitive advantage for his firm. The Network Computer (NC) had been introduced, and business analysts were predicting that it could presage the end of the PC. Dell didn't consider it a "new idea" at all – rather, he regarded it as "an updated version of the 'dumb terminal' of the 1980s." He questioned the predictions, believing instead that most PC users had become too dependent on their machines and would resist. Further, he already saw a future in which mobile computing would become more important. Consequently, Dell challenged the firm's product team to look beyond the NC to its underlying purpose and to identify a better solution, one in which Dell could play an active part. The solution was Managed PCs – that is, PCs with traditional features and flexibility familiar to PC users but that allow network administrators to configure, manage, and maintain hardware and software from a central location.

Managed PCs was a breakthrough idea – and most computer manufacturers have a version of their own – whereas NCs, to quote Dell, have become "roadkill on the information superhighway."

The moral behind the story is that employees need to be trained to confront strategic challenges and come up with the best answers fast. Employees must be taught to ask, "How can we do better? What can we do that no one yet does, that allows us to achieve our goal?"

This brings us to another element of Dell's approach to innovative thinking.

COMMUNICATE CORPORATE GOALS

It might seem too obvious to mention, but any effort at innovation demands that all employees know their company's strategic objectives, not to mention departmental or divisional objectives. If they aren't, their energies will be misdirected.

A manager myself, I can relate to this in terms of the more mundane issue of performance management – employees who have no insight into department or division goals can waste their time on the wrong efforts, something that can create conflict at assessment time. But this issue has broader impact if you think in terms of the creative energies of staff. At Dell, the objectives are simple: create the best possible customer experience and enhance shareholder value.

> Employees must be taught to ask, "How can we do better? What can we do that no one yet does, that allows us to achieve our goal?"

The firm uses quantitative measures to mark progress toward those goals, aligning individual performance against these strategic initiatives. Clearly this is part of the ownership culture previously mentioned but it also directs employee attention to question internal operations as much as customer needs and wants and leads to improvements in operations.

Earlier I mentioned the trend toward knowledge management. Whether so named or not, Dell has its own version, inculcated into its ownership culture, in which staff across the company share best practices as they ask questions of themselves and others across the company. Formal and informal, this process is very much a part of what Dell means when he talks about "teaching innovative thinking." But it would not be effective if employees did not fully understand either the firm's objectives or the underlying economic model from the standpoint of capital, supply chain, technology, and market trends. As Dell explains in his book, most employees can explain the fundamentals of the business because Dell spends lots of time communicating what's going on – not only what employees need to do to achieve the firm's goals but the objectives themselves and their implications. Each year, Dell chairs town hall meetings at which he discusses the firm's state of health, corporate strategies, market position, and plans for the future. Then, he answers questions.

These occasions also offer the opportunity to congratulate teams on their successes, which not only sustains motivation but also helps to share best practices. "One group benefits from what's working for others," Dell has told reporters.

Communication is very much a part of Dell's practice of innovative thinking. Says Dell, "Things happen in the morning that you have to react to by the afternoon. We have to be competitive 24 hours a day, 365 days a year, or else we lose business. A sense of urgency about communicating and solving problems is imperative."

DON'T IGNORE PROBLEMS – THEY DON'T GO AWAY

In his book *Direct from Dell,* Dell wryly cautions, "Don't try to perfume a pig." He's referring to the tendency of some organizations to pretend they don't smell the stink, or others that try to drown the smell warnings in corporate-speak or other counter-productive efforts. At Dell, when problems are encountered, they are fixed. In his book, Dell explains that, by don't perfume the pig, "we mean, 'Don't try to make something appear better than it really is.' Sooner or later the truth will come out, and you are better off dealing with it head on."

In part, Dell can do this because the facts are readily available. Given the model by which Dell operates – direct sales – the metrics are immediately accessible to management. "We receive constant information on everything, from our products to demand trends to quality data both in field performance and in our factories," Dell boasts to executives. Data are available on almost everything – from market demands to quality issues, to sales figures by sales rep from minute to minute. Dell even boasts that the organization maintains metrics on soft issues, like PR and human resources. Of course, the company's information includes customer feedback which provides opportunity for both self-improvement and learning.

Again, in keeping with "teaching innovative thinking," Dell and his management team encourage employees to ask "What's wrong?" then consider the issues and identify the solution quickly. "Our people know they are either part of the problem or part of the solution," says Dell. If they can't resolve the problem themselves, they also know they can seek help. But, most important, they know that problems, once identified, are more quickly solved.

So far, you may be thinking, "I've read some solid management advice – often discussed, infrequently practiced. But how has Dell come up with so many great product and marketing ideas?" The answer was touched on earlier, but it is a two-part reply.

ACCEPT THAT MISTAKES CAN OCCUR

Dell would be the first to admit that not all the decisions made by him have been the right ones. Likewise, he doesn't expect his employees to be right one hundred percent of the time. To encourage his employees to practice innovative thinking, within the culture of Dell is the clear message that mistakes are acceptable if they are learning experiences. If a team tries and fails but knows why it fails, says Dell, that's not failure. Rather, he believes, that it is an "important milestone on the road to achieving success." Companies that send a message to employees that mistakes are never forgotten aren't encouraging further innovation – just the opposite. They are teaching something about innovation – that innovation may be too risky to try.

PRACTICE SMART EXPERIMENTATION

In advocating innovation, it is important to realize that Dell is a believer in reasonable risk taking or "smart experimentation" as he describes it in his book. One such example was his decision to sell computers over www.dell.com. Dell had considerable opposition to this plan, yet he also had metrics that suggested that the idea would work. The same occurred as Dell grew his firm beyond the US borders. Although his decision to take his firm to the UK was risky, given again the predictions of failure from business analysts, he also had knowledge of the computer industry in that country to support his decision. When his decision proved successful, he was able to move beyond the UK to Canada and Germany and later to Sweden, France, and Japan. Most recently against opposition from analysts again, Dell chose to enter China, with considerable success. His current move is to Brazil. As Dell has said, "If you're smart about experimenting, it can lead to strategies that create new avenues of growth and ultimately become 'business as usual.' "

LEARNING INNOVATIVE THINKING FROM MICHAEL DELL

Michael Dell and his firm, he would say, practice "smart experimentation." This consists of the following steps:

◆ *Develop a culture for innovation.* A sense of ownership among employees encourages them to ask questions about the marketplace, customer needs, and operational issues. From such questions ideas often develop that can create competitive advantage.

◆ *Study, study, study.* As Dell observes learning, is a necessity. It is too easy to fall behind given the fast pace of change in the new millennium. To sustain the learning process, systems should be in place to provide metrics, as well as qualitative information, from which trends and developments can be discerned and potential problems identified.

◆ *Act to address problems*. Don't let a problem go untended. The sooner it is dealt with, the less the consequences on the bottom line.

◆ *Don't penalize failures*. So long as employees learn from their mistakes, they can be tolerated. Punishing those whose innovative efforts fail discourages not only those who failed but also their co-workers.

◆ *Take reasonable risks*. Decisions based on knowledge – qualitative and quantitative – are probably good ones. Even if they prove wrong, so long as you can learn from the experience, the effort is worthwhile.

BIBLIOGRAPHY

Dell, Michael and Fredman, Catherine, *Direct from Dell: Strategies That Revolutionized an Industry*, HarperBusiness, New York 1999.

Higgins James M., *Innovate or Evaporate: Test & Improve Your Organization's I.Q. (Innovation Quotient)*, New Management Publishing Company Inc., Winter Park, FL 1995.

Hodgetts, Richard, Luthans, Fred and Slocum, John Jr, "Strategy and HRM Initiatives for the '00s Environment: Redefining Roles and Boundaries, Linking Competencies and Resources," *Organizational Dynamics*, American Management Association New York City, Autumn 1999.

Leary, Banning Kent, "An 'Instinct' for Computer Success," *Nation's Business* April 1991.

Leonard, Dorothy and Swap, Walter, *When Sparks Fly: Igniting Creativity in Groups*, Harvard Business School Press, Cambridge, MA 1999.

Lipman-Blumen, Jean and Leavitt, Harold J., "Hot Groups 'with Attitude': A New Organizational State of Mind," *Organizational Dynamics*, Spring 1999, American Management Association, New York City.

Server, Andrew F., "Michael Dell Turns the PC World Inside Out," *Fortune*, September 8, 1997.

Eight

THINK AND ACT GLOBAL

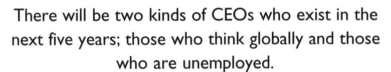

There will be two kinds of CEOs who exist in the next five years; those who think globally and those who are unemployed.
– Peter Drucker

Michael Dell early recognized the worth of taking Dell Computer Corporation global. The firm was only two and a half years old, and capital was scarce, but Dell and his management team knew that they had to expand their business beyond the US if it was to continue to grow. They studied likely markets and discarded several because they already were dominated by local businesses (like Japan) and passed up other, safer options because they didn't fit into longer-term plans (like Canada which, while prosperous, would not help Dell establish itself in Europe). Their final choice was the UK.

Dell had been there on vacation two years before. He had seen the same kind of high markup/service gap that existed in the US. Sales of computers were healthy but quality of merchandise was poor.

Dell reports in his book *Direct from Dell* that there was a supplier in the UK called Amstrad that sold what Dell refers to as a "disposable PC," an inexpensive model with a high failure rate and little service support. In Dell's opinion, Amstrad helped Dell by teaching potential purchasers of PCs not to buy low-end PCs with unreliable components and little service support. Consequently, Amstrad laid the foundation for Dell UK's subsequent success.

Dell UK opened for business in June 1987.

MOVE ABROAD ONE COUNTRY AT A TIME

Response by the British business press to the Dell move was negative. The general consensus was that direct sales would not work in the UK but customers proved wrong the reporters who predicted failure of the enterprise. Just the opposite happened. Dell UK was profitable from the beginning. Now it is almost a $1 billion-a-year business. And its success served as a springboard for further success in Europe and, ultimately, globally. Once it was successful in the UK, Dell moved into Canada and Germany. Thereafter, it moved into Sweden, France, and then into the Pacific-Rim and Japan.

GROW GLOBAL AS YOU GROW

It has been a little over ten years, and today Dell Computer has operations in North and South America, and the Asia-Pacific region. The Americas segment covers the US, Canada, and Latin America. The European segment is based in Bracknell, England, and covers the European countries and also some Middle Eastern and African nations. The Asia-Pacific/Japan segment covers the Pacific Rim, including Japan, Australia, and New Zealand; it is based in Hong Kong and Kawasaki, Japan.

The company has assembly facilities in Limerick (Ireland), Penang (Malaysia) and most recently Xiamen (China).

DELL'S GOLDEN RULES OF GLOBALIZATION

If you have yet to recognize that the world is global and that there are wonderful opportunities for those organizations that do business outside their own country, these guidelines based on Michael Dell's success may mean little. But for those who see that the issue is not whether to go global but how to do so to maximize success and minimize risk in these markets, these lessons from Dell's own global strategy will be of value:

◆ *Don't leap without looking.* Ruth Stanat, in her book *Global Gold,* warns that many mid-size and smaller firms' decision to go global is a "knee-jerk reaction" to press reports on "hot countries." Dell had several options, and he chose, as his first global effort, to enter the UK because he knew about the quality of product sold there, recognized the similarity between the US and UK computer markets, and believed that experience in the UK would best position his firm for its next international move, to Europe.

◆ *Select your global approach.* Despite the naysayers, Dell believed strongly, based on his homework, that his direct-sell approach would work in the UK and he was proved right. Since then, his firm has entered numerous other foreign markets, and in each instance, he has applied this approach with adaptations to suit cultural norms. His entry into one country after another has been part of a greater plan, based on regional market studies followed by more in-depth studies of each country.

◆ *Grow your global plan country by country.* Dell and his management team are firm believers in "ready, aim, shoot," not the "shotgun" approach in which the company enters an entire region at one time. While the latter may accelerate globalization efforts, it is a riskier approach. In particular, there is the danger of having to pull out of one country or two within the region which can impact business throughout the region.

◆ *Develop a global mentality.* Dell and his management team made a commitment to go global, and this may be one of the factors most important to the success of the firm's globalization. From 1987, the firm has included globalization as part of its strategic planning. One caveat that Dell might offer: *Globalization may fuel rapid growth that your firm may not be able to handle.* Consequently, stay domestic until you have the resources to spend, even if you are mentally ready for the move. Globalization demands capital and resources.

◆ *Maintain your product quality and service, service, service.* Bringing its suppliers abroad with it ensured that product produced outside the US would be equal to that manufactured in the US. Further, service operations around the world equal those offered US consumers. When you are competing in foreign markets, all you have is your reputation. And the world is growing smaller when it comes to communications about product or service quality – a poor reputation in one part of the world can spill over to other regions in the world.

DON'T CHANGE A GOOD THING, BUT ADAPT WHEN NEEDED

In each global expansion, Michael Dell recalls, the response was doubtful. The naysayers seemed to disappear after the firm's successful expansion into western and central Europe but then returned as the company moved into Asia. They argued that the direct-sell model was a Western concept and wouldn't work in the Pacific Rim. Again, Dell proved the naysayers wrong.

In *Direct from Dell,* Dell sounds very much like Percy Barnevik, the Swedish-born global executive, who said of his own firm, "We are not a global business. We are a collection of local businesses with intense global coordination." Dell points out the adaptations necessary to sell global – from the no-brainer's like recognizing you can't sell English-language computers in Russia to cultural issues like adapting marketing schemes in Germany, offering fax numbers to respond to ads, since Germans aren't comfortable telephoning in response to an ad. "They see it as too forward." The fax asks for the person's name and phone number so a Dell sales representative can call them. The subsequent conversation, then, is very much like one that would have occurred if the German customer had called himself or herself.

> They thought we were absolutely crazy."
> – Michael Dell recalling a brainstorming session in which he said that the company was going to expand internationally

But the direct-sell model in Germany and every other country is very much similar to that in the US. When local management didn't appreciate the purpose of the direct-sell model and tried to build a hybrid, Dell says, they didn't succeed. This is why Dell is very selective in those he hires to lead his foreign operations. In his opinion, you have to hire those who have embraced the company's vision. As history has proven, straying from that vision can be costly.

Internal sales figure prominently in Dell's bottom line. For instance, revenues from Asia-Pacific/Japan increased by 79 percent from 1997 to 1998 and an additional 37 percent from 1998 to 1999. Net revenues in the European segment experienced a growth of 50 percent in fiscal years 1999 and 1998, with growth across all customer groups and product lines.

Most recently Dell Computer expanded its global presence in two other countries: Italy and China. The decision to open a direct marketing, sales, and technical support facility in Milan did not generate as much interest as a similar move in Xiamen, China.

Already Dell has direct-to-customer operations in thirteen countries in the Asia-Pacific region. In February 1998, it announced it would establish a customer center in the world's most populous country, producing, selling, and providing service and technical support for the company's full range of computer systems from a 135,000 square-foot facility in the southern coastal city in China.

WHERE DO YOU WANT TO GO?

If you plan to take your company global, you can start by looking at the various regions to decide where you want to begin your internalization. Here is some information about world markets to begin your research:

◆ *Western Europe.* The 23 countries in Western Europe are among the most prosperous in the world, but not all countries are equally rich. For instance, the average per capita annual income in Portugal is $8700 compared with $36,900 in Switzerland. While there are also differences in family and work patterns, for the most part the once varied societies of Western Europe have become remarkably alike. Any firm interested in doing business in Western Europe needs to take into consideration the EU. Its creation has already made numerous changes, from creation of an improved infrastructure to creation of a community-wide labor pool. Any company planning to market to any country in this region or to the region itself should consider how it can best benefit from a unified Europe.

◆ *Eastern and central Europe.* On the plus side, Eastern bloc consumers are familiar with Western brand names and view them as being of higher quality than domestic products. But the downside includes not only the ethnic battles within the Balkan countries but also poor distribution infrastructure, underdeveloped wholesale market, insufficient and unattractive retail space, absence of self-service, and existence of what is called three-line system (to select, pay for, and pick up merchandise). These make shopping time-consuming and frustrating.

◆ *Asia/Pacific.* The 23 countries that make up the Pacific Rim region represent 56 percent of the world's population and account for 28 percent of global income in 1995. With the exception of the developed economies of Japan, Singapore, Hong Kong, and Australia, the Asia Pacific compares in economic growth to the post-World War II era for the US and Western Europe, according to Ruth Stanat. In her book *Global Gold,* Stanat offers a caveat: don't assume that the Asia-Pacific countries have similar cultures. Even within a single country such as China, she says, there are vast ethnic differences in the people throughout the country. She points to differences in political structures and different cultures but also to a long history of wars, economic struggles, and even hatreds between cultures. Consequently, she continues, a firm whose product does well in Japan should not make the assumption that the same product, let alone marketing campaign, will work in Hong Kong or South Korea.

◆ *Latin America*. This includes the Caribbean and Central and South America and Mexico. It is home to 480 million people, and is larger than Western Europe. There has been considerable interest in the countries of Latin America as balanced budgets have become a priority and government-sponsored efforts to eliminate barriers to foreign trade and investment are under way.

◆ *Middle East*. This includes 17 countries, accounts for 1.5 percent of 1995 GNP, has a total population of approximately 299 million, and has an annual per-capita income of $3690. In the past, the region reflected a pan-Arabism, a form of nationalism that amounted to anti-Western feelings. During the Persian Gulf War, this weakened, as the Gulf Arabs and their allies broke away to accept help from the US, an ally of Israel, in order to defeat Iraq. This is seen as a positive sign of market opportunities in the region for US firms.

◆ *Africa*. The African continent is so large that the US would fit about three and one half times. Actually, Africa is divided into three distinct areas: the Republic of South Africa, North Africa, and Black Africa located between the Sahara Desert in the north and Zambezi River in the south. A developing region, Africa has an annual per-capita income of $4700. Even the Republic of South Africa, known for its gold mines (about half of the area's exports) has a GNP per capita of only $2800. Within the region as a whole the problems are the same: slow growth and low investment. Even the mines of South Africa are winding down. The challenge for businesses interested in this region is not to stimulate demand for products but to identify the most important needs and develop products that satisfy them.

"This move places us closer to our customers in a market that presents excellent long-term growth opportunities for Dell," said Mort Topfer, vice-chairman. "The expansion in China is a real milestone for our company."

Only two years earlier, the firm had announced its increased investment in the Asia-Pacific region with offices in six countries and construction on a major manufacturing facility in Malaysia. The Malaysia facilities are now the hub of a comprehensive Asia-Pacific management, sales, and marketing network that includes Australia, China, Eastern Russia, Hong Kong, India, Indonesia, Korea, Malaysia, New Zealand, Pakistan, the Philippines, Singapore, Taiwan, and Thailand. And now the company has operations in China.

> "If you haven't begun to expand your business outside your local country, you are missing 'the golden gold rush.'"
> – **Ruth Stanat,**
> *Global Gold*

BRING SUPPLIERS ABROAD WITH YOU

As the company has expanded over the world, it has also added an element to its direct-sell model to make for easier management of the process. Dell expresses this idea in two words: "Proximity pays." In essence, the company determined that it was less costly to purchase supplies from those suppliers near its plants. So, Dell explains, his company went to its suppliers and told them that if they wanted to continue to be the firm's supplier, then they must develop the capability to serve Dell around the world. So a vendor who supplied products to the manufacturing facility in Ireland would have to build a manufacturing facility near the firm's plant in Penang and another next to its plant in China. When Dell grew its operation at Round Rock, Texas, the same company added a plant there.

SEE THE BIGGER PICTURE

Any discussion of Dell's global operations must recognize that as early as 1987 Dell had the mindset to go global. He didn't see operations in one or more foreign countries as a sideline but as an integral part of his firm's future. As smaller and mid-size firms of today recognize that expansion will mean a global presence, Dell knew that his firm's future expansion would depend on gaining footholds in all regions of the world. That mindset continues to exist at Dell.

Like many executives today, in the beginning Dell had to address some serious concerns:

◆ Did his company have the financial resources to handle an overseas venture when they were stretching domestic resources?

◆ Was the risk too big for a company less than three years old?

◆ Could the business sustain an overseas operation in the UK (and later in other parts of the world) until there was a sufficient payback?

◆ Most importantly, would the same market approach – direct-sell – work in the UK and around the world as successfully as it had worked in the United States?

On the other hand, Dell's brief visit to the UK and subsequent study clearly indicated that the same problems with the computer industry existed there that existed in the US, thereby providing a relatively safe test country to begin his growth plans. Dell's global strategy led him initially to developed countries but, over time, has taken him into emerging markets like the Asia-Pacific countries, including China. But taking his business model abroad also meant the opportunity to improve profitability. Dell reasoned, and wisely, that if he didn't capitalize on market opportunities in the global marketplace, his competitors from the US would do so. Once local consumers switch their brand preferences from local suppliers to your competitors, entering the market becomes a greater challenge, since you have to face not only local providers but also existing competitors already entrenched in the market.

Going global also gave him insights into competitors from around the world.

If you think broadly about going abroad, it is evident that globalization is an obvious move for most firms since it addresses many of their basic issues, like:

◆ new customers;

◆ a larger market;

◆ customer retention, as you learn from foreign market experience and competitors;

◆ best management practices;

◆ provision of technology upgrades to satisfy customer needs
   around the world; and

◆ new marketing techniques to reach a worldwide market.

Thus, going global positions well a business to survive and grow,
even during market swings. But going global isn't easy. On the
other hand, a key rule of international business is "keep it
simple," as Ruth Stanat notes in her book *Global Gold, Panning
for Gold in Foreign Markets*. Stanat observes that an important
rule to follow is to make sure that people at all levels of the
firm know the global strategy. Also, as Dell would add, be certain that they are ready to follow that strategy. As he learned,
those that attempted to adapt his direct-sell strategy beyond
cultural adaptations failed.

BE ALERT TO MARKET ADAPTATIONS, NOT JUST LANGUAGE

Most executives are familiar with the need to pay attention to
the language of the foreign country in which they enter. The
story about how Pepsi's advertisement "Come alive with Pepsi"
translated in German as "Come out of the grave with Pepsi" is
well known. So is the fact that Schweppes' tonic water translated into Italian as *Il Water*, i.e. "the bathroom." So most companies going global pay attention to marketing copy. Equally
important is the marketing strategy. A successful marketing
approach in one country will not *automatically* work in another
country. An example is the 800 numbers that customers in the
US use to order from Dell but the *fax* numbers that customers

in Germany demand. Countries and peoples of the world differ from one another. Customer preferences, competitors, channels of distribution, and communication media may differ. Any
firm that plans to go global needs to learn the extent to which
marketing plans and programs can be extended worldwide, as
well as the extent to which they must be adapted. A phrase has
developed that reflects this, "Think globally and act locally."

A decision to enter a foreign market must be preceded by studies into:

◆ local competition;

◆ current distribution channels and marketing strategies by
  local companies;

◆ comparison of local products or services with those you will
  offer;

◆ consumer attitude toward the product or service you plan to
  offer;

◆ local skills and abilities and location to help to determine
  on-site location of your facilities; and

◆ sourcing – Dell's approach being to take his suppliers with
  him and manufacture in various regions of the world. But
  other firms prefer to manufacture in their home country, a
  strategy that may alienate local customers if there are strong
  nationalistic feelings in the country in which they plan to
  market their product. These individuals put a positive value
  on the feature "Made in [home country]."

In each instance in which Dell has gone abroad, it has undertaken these kinds of studies before locating operations in a country or region. When Dell has entered a region it has been prepared to stay, knowledgeable that those firms that enter a market, then withdraw, then try to enter again have had a very hard time regaining market interest. According to Stanat, if there is any part of the world with long memories it is Latin America. Stanat, the founder and president of SIS International Research, observes in her book that withdrawal from one Latin country can have the impact of a "disease" on Latin American operations, as market attitude toward the firm in one country spreads to other countries in the region due to connection of countries through trade pacts (Mercosur, NAFTA, and the like).

> "Of 22 journalists who came to the press announcement, all but one predicted that the firm would fail ... The business was profitable from the very first days, and now Dell UK is almost a $2 billion a year company."
> **– Michael Dell, recalling the start of the UK operation**

Dell's initial entry into globalization may have been based on a brief trip to the UK with family and a general idea about other regional markets. But subsequent decisions have been well thought out, following major research about markets.

Plans are currently under way to expand operations in Brazil.

BIBLIOGRAPHY

Dell, Michael and Fredman, Catherine, *Direct from Dell: Strategies That Revolutionized an Industry*, HarperBusiness, New York 1999.

Burton, Kate, "The Rise and Rise of Dell-Boy," *Computer Weekly*, July 8, 1993.

Larry, Banning Kent. "An 'Instinct' for Computer Success," *Nation's Business*, April 1991.

Stanat, Ruth, *Global Gold: Panning for Profits in Foreign Markets*, AMACOM, a division of American Management Association International, New York 1998.

Nine

STAY TRUE TO YOUR TALENTS

Imagination is a good horse to carry you over the
ground – not a flying carpet to set you free from
probability.
– Robertson Davies

It's hard to be a successful entrepreneur in today's times. Society expects you to keep breaking new ground, finding new ways of being successful to prove that the first time wasn't just a fluke.

Sometimes the pressure to repeat the first success is so great that an entrepreneur loses sight of those corporate competencies that made the business a success in the first place. He or she begins to move in a direction 180 degrees different from the first success. This isn't to say that an organization shouldn't undertake continuous improvement, even a process of corporate renewal, in response to changes in its industry or market. But the desire to exceed the first accomplishment shouldn't lead an executive to stray from those strengths that made that first effort a success.

When Dell Computer went public in 1984, it had three corporate strengths:

◆ the direct model;

◆ recognition of the importance of listening to customers; and

◆ disdain for stockpiling inventory.

Those three corporate competencies have undergone refreshment to reflect changes that have occurred in the years since, but they continue to be the foundation of the business. Dell did stray from that successful triad. It didn't discourage him from exploring new business opportunities, but the experiences, early in the company's history, did teach him the importance, as an executive, of a firm sticking to what it is good at.

WHAT HAPPENED TO TEACH HIM THIS MANAGERIAL LESSON?

The most significant situation involved Dell's direct model. From 1990 through 1992, the company had enjoyed tremendous growth. Caught up with the excitement, Dell and his management team decided that it was time to emulate other computer firms and sell products through the retail channel, in addition to selling directly to customers by phone. Two years later, Dell abandoned the retail channel. It had just announced that its computers would be sold in Wal-Mart, but it had also done a P&L on the retail business as part of an overall analysis of the business. The information indicated that Dell was, indeed, successfully selling PCs through stores like CompUSA and Circuit City, but it also showed that the company wasn't actually making any money on the sales. Money was going to the chains. Nothing could be done in terms of design to reduce production costs to turn a profit for Dell.

> "If your business isn't enabled by providing customers and suppliers with more information, you're probably already in trouble."
> – **Michael Dell**

Despite adverse publicity about its decision – Dell recalls that financial writers said the company would stunt its growth by

MICHAEL DELL AND W. EDWARDS DEMING

Michael Dell may never have met W. Edwards Deming, but his organization clearly demonstrates the fourteen points that constitute the heart and soul of Deming's approach to management.

1. *Strive for continuous improvement.* Yes, Dell Computer is founded on three competencies but this hasn't kept the organization from striving for continuous improvement in products and services.
2. *Use resources wisely.* Dell's sharing of information with suppliers ensures that its plants practice JIT inventory management.
3. *Build quality in from the very beginning.* Dell maintains a vendor quality program that demands that suppliers meet specific quality standards.
4. *Build a relationship with a few key suppliers.* Dell knows that searching for lowest-cost suppliers only creates production inconsistencies and quality problems. Rather, he believes in building long-term loyal, and trusting relationships with a small group of suppliers.
5. *Prevent recurrence of problems; better yet, keep problems from occurring.* This is behind regular senior management think-tanks and factory team meetings.
6. *Train the workforce.* Dell builds work teams that make sure each of their members has a clear idea of how to do their job.
7. *Provide real leadership.* That leadership starts at the top – with Michael Dell himself. But each of the divisions and work groups have leaders who can provide individualized help.

8. *Provide opportunities for employees to ask questions about why and how.* As Deming observed, employees do things wrong when they are afraid to ask questions.
9. *Promote teamwork.* At Dell, employees are organized into teams. The flow of information across corporate boundaries further supports the sense of teamwork throughout the organization.
10. *Provide tools to monitor results.* Slogans don't do the job. Facts and figures against which managers can measure performance raise productivity.
11. *Have goals and standards by which performance is measured.* These give purpose to the work.
12. *Encourage pride in workmanship.* Dell looks to do away with those obstacles that impede quality performance: e.g. inadequate instruction, faulty equipment, poor supervision (see Chapter 4).
13. *Provide opportunities for employee stretch.* Greater knowledge means greater opportunities for employees – and increased productivity for the company.
14. *The customer always comes first.* Deming wrote in *Out of the Crisis,* "The consumer is the most important part of the production line. Quality should be aimed at the needs of the consumer, present and future."

getting out of retail – and there was even internal opposition to the decision, Dell withdrew from retail and refocused corporate attention on direct sales. Since products sold direct and those sold retail demanded different specifications, the decision actually simplified production. In Dell's opinion, it refocused attention on the direct model which was the basis for the firm's success in the first place.

In talking to *Harvard Business Review,* Michael Dell said, "I don't think we knew how far the direct model could take us. It has provided a consistent underlying strategy for Dell despite a lot of change in our industry. Along the way, we have learned a lot." In particular, he noted how it allowed the firm to leverage its relationships with both suppliers and customers to the extent that he could use the term "virtual integration." He went on to suggest that virtual integration allowed him to build a much larger business much more quickly – that he couldn't have created a business as large if it had been vertically integrated.

Likewise, the desire to grow the business at a faster rate led to violation of another Dell operating rule: *demand/supply.* In 1989 the company bought more memory chips than it needed in anticipation of the sales it expected. Not only did they buy the chips based on an exaggerated forecast but they bought them when prices were volatile. Right after Dell's purchase, prices fell. Even worse, technologically the chips were useless almost immediately thereafter as memory-chip capacity went from 256k to 1 megabyte. Dell was left with chips that had cost "a ton of money" and that no one had use for, so the firm couldn't resell them.

Thereby, experience taught Michael Dell the importance of inventory velocity. Tangential to this was Dell's early realization that it should purchase parts from others rather than be in the business of building computers from scratch itself. According to Dell, this went very much against the dominant thinking of the time. "The IBMs, Compaqs, and HPs subscribed to a 'we-have-to-develop-everything" viewpoint," he told the press. But Dell didn't see success in placing small semiconductor chips on printed circuit boards. Rather, value came from selection of top-quality suppliers who could do this, freeing Dell to put its capital into efforts that would add value to its customers. "I'm not saying those activities aren't important. They need to get done very, very well. But they're not sources of value that Dell is going to create," he told *Harvard Business Review*.

The third lesson may seem the oddest given the firm's customer-focus. No question, Dell listens to its customers and it responds to market demands and needs. But early on in the firm's history, Dell forgot to listen. In essence, Dell decided for its customers that they would want certain technological features. Shown the features, customers weren't impressed, but Dell chose to show them at a trade show in 1989. Given the public's indifferent response, the product idea was dropped. The company had let its own enthusiasm direct its actions rather than its customers' interests – a matter, Dell has said, of "technology for technology's sake rather than technology for the customer's sake."

Michael Dell now finds ways to listen to his customers, like the Platinum Councils held twice a year in each major region of the world. About 100 members from the company's senior management and key people from engineering and development teams meet with corporate customers to share concerns and to discuss anticipated technology changes. Said Dell, "The purpose of these Platinum Councils is clearly for us to listen."

So the lessons have taught Dell the value of finding its edge and then sticking to that within the constraints of today's ever-changing world. Speaking to a group of businessmen in San Francisco in spring 1999, Michael Dell said his firm had spent the years since it was founded refining its core capabilities: "a custom-build process for both hardware and software integration that brings cost efficiencies to Dell and its customers, a personalized customer relationship process that allows us to provide ever greater levels of service customization," and a well developed infrastructure for high-volume order management and continuous flow logistics. He attributed Dell Computer's ability to sell to – and service – new customer segments and expand geographically, as well as introduce successfully new product categories to this three-part formula.

> "As much as anything, the linchpin that makes it all work is Dell's competence in manufacturing."
> – **John H. Sheridan,**
> *Industry Week*

This is not to say that Dell has not adapted the formula as opportunities arise, as his adaptation of the direct model to the Internet direct model demonstrates. In Michael Dell's view, the Internet was a natural way for his firm to communicate with its customers and provide support information. "There's nothing more direct than letting customers configure their own system in real time and giving them an order confirmation right away," Dell told a reporter for *Industry Week*. In his opinion the Web offers "a whole new level of intimacy with customers." This is not only in terms of sales. Dell has created more than 60,000 password-protected customized customer Web pages, "Premier Pages," containing information and purchase-order processes unique to corporate customers. These Premier Pages contain the same service and support information as the databases of Dell's own technicians and engineers." No wonder, the company receives 400,000 weekly e-mails for service and support, compared with 165,000 weekly phone calls for the same service and support.

But, as Dell has told audiences of businesspeople around the world, online commerce represents only a small part of the Internet's value to companies that he labels "Internet revolutionaries." In his opinion, its real value lies in its ability to change traditional relationships between suppliers, vendors, and customers. Those companies that use the Internet to do this – that make the Internet an integral part of their strategy – not just an add on – have the potential to "fundamentally change the face of global competition," Dell told *Industry Week*. Dell was referring to the customized Web pages for its 25-or-so suppliers that allow these firms to provide Dell with real-time information on capacities, capabilities, and component quality as measured by Dell's metric and cost structures. And Dell, in turn, provides suppliers with information from customers – gathered from its Premier Pages and from semi-annual customer councils – on product quality, future demand, technical requirements, and market pricing. In the opinion of the founder of Dell, the Web really boosts the value of information sharing. "We can share design databases and methodologies with supplier-partners in ways that just weren't possible five to ten years ago. This speeds time to market, dramatically – and creates a lot of value that can be shared between buyer and supplier."

> "Much of Dell's success comes from continued innovation and improvement of its direct marketing formula."
> **– Joseph E. Maglitta,**
> *Electronic Business*

Just as Dell continues to practice the direct model, albeit now on the Web, he also continues to be concerned about maintaining a highly efficient manufacturing facility. This explains Metric 12, a 265,000 square foot manufacturing facility with state-of-the-art equipment. The two-storey facility north of Austin doubles Dell's US manufacturing capacity. According to Ro Parra, a Dell senior vice-president, the factory was designed to achieve high-inventory velocity, flexibility, and simplicity in the flow of materials. "In this factory, we were able to take what we'd learned over several years and apply what we think are state-of-the-art manufacturing technologies to deliver value to the marketplace," he told reporters. Typical manufacturing cycle time is now slightly more than one day including testing. One key to the direct-shipment capability of Metric 12 as well as flow of material through the plant is the provision of 52 dock-doors, used for delivery and shipping. Orders come in about every 20 seconds, making collaboration among work teams critical. The Dell plant addresses the issue with weekly meetings of production, supply-manage and channel-manage personnel. "They meet face to face," according to Keith Maxwell, a senior vice-president of the firm's Americas manufacturing organization, "and they talk about supply demand issues, upsides and downsides, and how to adjust to balance the two."

Also unique is the fact that plant suppliers have on-site resident planners who manage their own inventory on a replenishment basis. Planning information is shared weekly with key suppliers, who also have access to such information as daily consumption rates via the secure Web pages maintained by Dell. According to another Dell executive, Dell's goal is to have an electronic feed of day-to-day and hour-to-hour consumption.

DON'T MESS WITH SUCCESS

Michael Dell doesn't believe that "if it ain't broke, don't fix it." On the other hand, he also has learned since founding Dell that you don't mess with success. If there are some rules that Dell would share, they are:

◆ *Learn from your experiences.* Mistakes are opportunities – if we look at them as such – to perfect our management practices.

◆ *Rely on facts.* Whether we're talking about sales figures or customer input, they are important for making judgments, especially decisions that are critical to the hypergrowth of a business like Dell.

◆ *Adapt corporate competencies to changing times.* While it's important to stay on course, alterations to that course may be necessary, as in the case of the Web making such a major change to our economy. Dell has adapted the communication opportunities with customers and suppliers from the Web to his direct-model, customer-focused firm, and supply-management chain. As he points out, information has always been important – the Web provides greater and more immediate access to it.

◆ *Fully leverage the Web.* Given the importance that Dell puts on the role of the Web, it deserves to be listed separately in this task list for corporate success. Dell has said, "The Web creates dramatic new opportunities and destroys old competitive advantages."

BIBLIOGRAPHY

Dell, Michael and Fredman, Catherine, *Direct from Dell: Strategies That Revolutionized an Industry*, HarperBusiness, New York 1999.

Dell, Michael, "DirectConnect," speech at Austin, August 25, 1999.

Dell, Michael, "Building the Infrastructure for 21st Century Commerce," speech at Las Vegas, May 12, 1999.

Dell, Michael, "The Dynamics of the Connected Economy," speech at Atlanta, June 25, 1999.

Dell, Michael, "Building a Competitive Advantage in an Internet Economy," speech at Detroit, November 1, 1999.

Dell, Michael, "The Foundation of E-Business," speech at San Francisco, February 15, 2000.

Maglitta, Joseph E., "Special Dell-ivery," *Electronic Business*, December 1997.

Magretta, Joan, "The Power of Virtual Integration: an Interview with Dell Computer's Michael Dell," *Harvard Business Review*, March–April 1998.

Sheridan, John H., "Focused on Flow," *Industry Week*, October 18, 1999.

Verespej, Michael. "Michael Dell's Magic," *Industry Week*, November 16, 1998.

Ten

MANAGE
HYPERGROWTH

You don't leap a chasm in two bounds.
– Chinese philosopher

Contrary to what people say, Michael Dell believes that, as a firm gets larger, growth doesn't slow. But, then, Dell may just be talking about his own company. In each of the first eight years of the company's existence it grew 80 percent; from 1992 through 1998 it grew 55 percent annually. In 1999 the company's growth was around 30 percent growth.

RECOGNIZE THAT GROWTH HAS ITS RISKS

No question, this kind of growth – Dell calls it "hypergrowth" – can be exciting. But the hectic pace it engenders can also lead to management mistakes. In his book *Warp-Speed Growth: Managing the Fast-Track Business Without Sacrificing Time, People, and Money*, Peter Meyer, founder of the consulting firm The Meyer Group, points out, "Growth can save you. Growth can drive you crazy: It can spurt and sputter; it can be sustainable. But it can also kill your business."

Consequently, rapid growth needs a strong executive at the corporate ship's helm – someone like Michael Dell who practices what Meyer characterizes as "sane management of growth."

As you review article after article written about Michael Dell since he founded his company, two terms repeatedly appear. One is "consummate salesman," often used in the early years of Dell Computer to describe Dell. At a 1997 shareholder meeting, he was compared to a politician on the campaign trail, shaking hands and patting shoulders as he mounted the dais to show investors a slide of his company's success over the past three years. The chart compared Dell stock with that of its six biggest competitors. The upward slope of the Dell line was twice as steep as the others. Dell reportedly looked over the crowd, paused, then grinned and said, "And that concludes our presentation."

Entrepreneurs have to be consummate sales people to make their visions a reality.

RECOGNIZE THE IMPORTANCE OF EXECUTION

But there is much more to Michael Dell. That became evident as the company took wings and began to grow. Another and more important side of Dell became evident – he is an eminent executor of operating efficiencies. Dell and his management team are constantly rethinking operations. When problems arise, he told an audience, "We ask ourselves how can we design that so it doesn't occur or how can we improve the process to prevent that from happening."

In 1993, an article in *Security Management* described how Dell Computer, as it expanded, had to strengthen corporate security, using the latest electronic technology and staffing with a strategic mix of proprietary and contract officers. After describing in depth the system installed by Dell, Dell Security Manager Robert L. Ansley concluded that Dell "has learned that the cheapest solution is not always the best solution; it is better to pay a few extra dollars to have the quality needed with expandability built in." Thereby, he reinforced the message of many reporters of the Dell story, pointing to execution as the

KEYS TO THE KINGDOM

To create and extract value with information – a key part of the Dell past, present, and future strategy for growth – executives must turn to the virtual world of the marketspace. Writing in *Harvard Business Review*, Jeffrey F. Rayport and John J. Sviokla, associate professor of business administration in the Service Management Unit of Harvard Business School and associate professor in the Management Information Systems Area at Harvard, respectively, point out that companies must pay attention to how their companies create value not only in the physical world but also the virtual world, which they call the marketspace. The value chain in the physical world is a series of value-adding activities that connect a company's supply side with its demand side. Analysis of this chain enables managers to redesign their internal and external processes to improve efficiency and effectiveness.

The physical value chain treats information as a "supporting element" of the value-adding process, not as a source of value itself, which is the case in the virtual world, write the two Harvard professors. They give the example of how managers use information that they capture on inventory, production, or logistics to help monitor or control those processes. "They rarely use information itself to create new value for the customer." This was what Federal Express did when it allowed customers to track packages through the company's Web site. After a package has been delivered, the sender can even identify the name of the person who signed for it. It's a free service from FedEx, adding value to the customer and thereby increasing loyalty. The authors exhort companies to look to the marketspace. Another case in point is MCA's music division. As the Web has made it possible for musicians to record, edit, and distribute their music directly over the Web or through commercial online services, MCA has chosen to build a site on the Web devoted to its label's bands and use the site to distribute digital audio and video samples and to provide information on band tours. To quote Rayport and John J. Sviokla, the site has become the division's "showroom" and in time will become a new retail channel. Further, the site can be used to search for new talent rather than audition bands in a studio, and edit and modify music on a computer rather than record take after take with a band to get the final master.

But taking this step further (*à la* Dell), the division might gain potential audience input, inviting fans to sit in on the Internet and listen as engineers edit the material or download interviews with the band's members before they are distributed more widely, building a new kind of relationship with customers.

Needless to say, creating value in the virtual chain does not mean not exploiting the value chain in the real world – a company "must play in both space and place," the authors observe. Managers must continue to oversee the physical value chain – making and selling CDs most efficiently – but they must also build and exploit the virtual value chain. How do you go about the latter?

"Creating value in any stage of a virtual value chain," they explain, "involves a sequence of five activities: gathering, organizing, selecting, synthesizing, and distributing information. Just as someone takes raw material and refines it into something useful – as in the sequence of tasks involved in assembling an automobile on a production line – so a manager today collects raw information and adds value through these steps."

strong point not only of its leader but also a part of the corporate culture.

Andrew Grove of Intel says of Dell, "He tackles jobs others think are overwhelming and prevails." Grove believes that "Dell has always been able to figure out the next wrinkle to stay ahead. It's in their genes." Asked about Compaq's and other competitors' move into direct selling, Dell isn't flummoxed. He believes he has a huge head start. "We already have a quick-ship plan for large customers where we can deliver a machine within 48 hours of an order," he told reporters.

A solid executor seems to be how Dell thinks of himself, too. In a *Fortune* interview in 1997, Dell told the reporter, "I'm no Larry Ellison," referring to the quotable CEO of Oracle. Nor would he seem to be a titan of technology *à la* Bill Gates, suggested *Fortune* reporter Andrew E. Serwer, "If his company's products are derided as commodities – boxes, nothing more – and his business model, of direct sales to customers, as déclassé, well, so be it. He's got two other things on his mind – his customers and his competitors." Dell likes to talk to his engineers and he spends time checking out innovations at tech facilities, but he spends lots more time with customers. Such contacts don't mean sales; rather, they mean keeping on top of an ever-changing market.

VALUE STRATEGIC INNOVATION

Another term for Michael Dell might be "value innovator," based on the definition of the term by W. Chan Kim and Renee Mauborgne, (Boston Consulting Group Bruce D. Henderson Chair Professor of Strategy and International Management at INSEAD and fellow and affiliate professor of Strategy and Management at INSEAD, respectively). In their article in *Harvard Business Review* published in a collection by Harvard

Press , the two INSEAD professors ask why some companies are able to sustain high growth in revenues and profits (think Dell). After studying more than 30 companies around the world, they found that the difference between high-growth companies and their less successful competitors lay in each firm's assumptions about strategy. "Managers of the less successful companies followed conventional strategic logic." In the authors' opinion, managers of the high-growth companies practiced what they called "the logic of value innovation." What's that?

"You know, there are still people who don't get it. They think that we're just a niche company serving a small group of customers. How could that be, if we're growing faster than anyone? That's not a claim – it's the truth."
– **Michael Dell,**
Fortune, 1997

Many companies let their competitors set the parameters of their strategic thinking where value innovators don't benchmark their thinking about the customers' needs against their rivals' thinking. Nor do value innovators take industry's conditions as given. They don't view opportunities through the perspective of existing capabilities and needs. Rather, value innovators ask, "What if we start anew?" Besides Dell, with its direct model, consider Virgin Atlantic that challenged industry conventions by eliminating first-class service and channeling savings into innovations for business passengers. And with Dell, we can't forget virtual integration and Dell.com.

FOUR FALLACIES OF GROWTH

In his book *Warp-Speed Growth: Managing the Fast-Track Business Without Sacrificing Time, People, and Money,* Peter Meyer, president of the Meyer Group, Scotts Valley, California, identifies four beliefs associated with growth that are incorrect.

♦ *You can grow out of an operational problem.* Take high costs. Volume may improve product costs, but the problem will still exist until something is done. Dell found that hypergrowth created problems that had to be managed, if not anticipated and prevented in advance.

♦ *Growth equals profitability.* Not necessarily so. Growth demands trade-offs that may reduce profits. For example, if growth comes from new customers, you can lose money if it costs you more to get these additional customers than the ones you already have.

♦ *Profitability improves when every customer is yours.* Meyer cites a study by Don Potter of Windermere Associates. In each of 240 lines of business, the top four competitors were identified. Potter found that only 29 percent of the market leaders were also the profitability leaders. For instance, Steelcase leads the market in office furniture but HON leads in profits. Wal-Mart may be dominant in its niche but Family Dollar and Dollar General are more profitable. Meyer explains, "Market leaders have to stretch to get the extra customers." That stretch can result in lower profits.

♦ *If you grow, customers will benefit.* The opposite is true, says Meyers. Yes, growth may enable you to offer new products or expand geographically, and thereby gain new customers, but those customers might have been gained at a lower cost without growth. "Every second of time that you invest in your own growth for its own sake is time that your business could have invested in customers, and they know it." Money from growth should be applied to improve the total customer experience.

BE PRACTICAL

In his book, *Direct from Dell,* Dell recalls the early months of Dell Computer when the fledgling firm experienced continuous change as a consequence of its rapid but youthful growth. Fortunately, the firm's founder resolved issues that arose in those early days in "a very practical way." Each time the company was faced with an issue, the question was asked, as it continues to be asked, "What's the most efficient way to accomplish this?" This approach not only made those first few months more manageable but also had a longer-term effect by creating the kind of team-oriented culture in which employees worked together to see the company succeed. Dell recalls, for instance, how members of the firm's first sales force had to set up their own computer systems. Not only, he says, did that eliminate the likelihood of bureaucracy cropping up then – and likely now, too – but it also made the very same people who would be marketing the computers alert to the kinds of problems future customers would experience undertaking the same tasks.

There wasn't much office space and money was tight, but each of the firm's early goals that were achieved sustained the enthusiasm of Dell and his first management team. But investors questioned whether Dell was just a young man who happened to be in the right place in the right time and got lucky. At Dell itself, more seemed to be happening than Dell himself could keep track of. At the same time, pressure was on to go public. In 1986, Dell called a brainstorming meeting of business leaders inside and outside the industry, in addition to corporate executives, to determine how best to evolve the business. From that meeting came some action plans:

◆ targeting large companies as clients;

◆ providing support with on-site service;

◆ taking the company global (first stop, the UK);

◆ reducing dealer markups by sustaining the direct relationship marketing concept that was fundamental to the company's startup;

◆ increasing inventory velocity via JIT (just-in-time) to maintain efficient, effective production.

That meeting was critical not only because of the decisions themselves but the fundamental impact that it had on Dell Computer. It began a pattern of goal setting that continues to this day and is critical to any organization experiencing hypergrowth as Dell continues to encounter.

One year later, Dell Computer went public. Its entry into the UK had proven successful, contrary to doomsayers' forecast that the direct model wouldn't work outside the US. At the time, the company's value was $85 million. As Dell writes in his own book, "We had done this in three years, starting with an idea and $1,000." What Dell doesn't mention is that the significant growth was carefully managed following competencies identified during the brainstorming session and pre-public offering meetings.

As yet, the company had not learned fully that with every growth opportunity comes an element of risk. Peter Meyer writes that warp-speed growth can have its dangerous side. From the late 1980s to early 1990s, Dell learned that lesson too well. Between 1989 and 1993, the company's sales grew from $389 million to $2.9 billion, but little was done to increase its management structure. The firm was unable to track profits and losses by product segment, and as the business expanded, the hands-on Dell found he was losing control of the ever-growing business. "We'd have meetings and everyone in the room would say we're doing great," Dell told one reporter, "and then you'd look at the numbers and there were problems. We had businesses that were performing extremely well and businesses that were performing extremely poorly, but nobody really knew which was which." The decision to sell retail, plus direct, proved a miscalculation when the numbers were carefully studied. Middlemen fees were cutting into the narrow margins and while sales were good, there were no profits.

"Sustained growth is seldom straightforward. It thrives best in an atmosphere that is tolerant of misjudgments – one that allows for standing back, learning from failures and being willing to try something new again."
– Robert M. Tomasko, Go for Growth

U.S. News & World Report wrote that 1993 was a year when Dell's "youth became a liability, a year when the financial analysts crowed their I-told-you so, and a year when the 29-year-old computer entrepreneur … saw his company cope with failure for the first time." The company's management problems had caused it to cancel its entire notebook computer line, missing out on a potential major market.

LESSONS LEARNED FROM EXPERIENCING HYPERGROWTH

In a meeting in September 1998 in Dallas, Michael Dell shared his formula for surviving supergrowth.

◆ *Ally with employees.* He told the group that Dell is aggressive in its recruiting the best talent it can find and designing jobs to accommodate hypergrowth. For instance the company will divide up people's jobs, something that sometimes doesn't go over too well. But, as Dell told the group, "six months later, because of growth, their job is the same size it was before, and they say, 'Please cut my job in half, I've got too much!' "

◆ *Be on the lookout for changes in the game.* Dell told the group how 12 years earlier he had invented something called on-site service, now pretty common in the industry, to provide personal computer service. The Internet is clearly a massive breakthrough in the way Dell products are sold (see Chapter 5, "Market Innovate"). Still another example of Dell's innovative practices is its sales force and system engineering force out in the field tied together by a centralized database.

◆ *Learn from your mistakes.* "We can be proud of having made mistakes and learning from them," he told the group. The foundation for success is not having all the answers but rather learning from your mistakes and not repeating them – and making sure that the lessons learned are shared throughout the organization as it grows.

◆ *Manage growth.* This may be the most important lesson that Dell could share with the eager-beaver audience of senior executives who might believe that there is no such thing as a company growing too fast. But as Dell said, "There is a level of growth that is not only too fast but dangerous and deadly to a company." He pointed out how Dell Computer had grown one year from $890 million in sales to $2.1 billion in sales. "It was thrilling and exciting," he admitted, but the following year the firm, he said, "hit the wall in a spectacular fashion and splintered into thousands of pieces." The experience taught them some lessons: how to understand the profitability of different parts of its business, where the business was successful and where it wasn't, and how to anticipate and build an infrastructure to support growth.

◆ *Remember that the customer is always right.* This mindset has not changed since the firm was founded. In 1991, it ranked number one in a customer-satisfaction survey. The company has grown 25 or more times the size then, and it still ranks number one, he told the audience.

◆ *Set up metric to monitor performance.* Dell uses ROIC (return on invested capital) and watches it carefully to ensure that it is creating value for shareholders.

◆ *Segment the business.* As Dell explained, his company sells to large customers, to global customers and to consumers. And each of these businesses has different characteristics – and different support costs, margins, levels of investment, capital intensities. By segmenting, Dell can both better service the different businesses, and measure performance and make tough business decisions.

◆ *Practice global expansion as a growth strategy.* Dell began its global expansion in the UK and since has moved out across Europe into central Europe, into Canada, Japan, Australia, Asia Pacific, Malaysia China, and Brazil. Experience has proven that the direct model is not exclusive to the English language or American culture but economics. And, Dell told his audience, "the economics work whether you're in Beijing or Boston, Barcelona or Botswana."

◆ *Don't practice "me-too" management.* You can't follow the other firms. You need to find your own way to do things better. That doesn't mean not adapting other organizations' ideas, but you should not allow your firm to be held to so-called industry conventions (e.g., retail versus the direct model).

◆ *Be out front in key trends.* Certainly Dell has demonstrated how to use the Internet beyond online sales. Further, while it could offer several different kinds of UNIX and also have NT, it would have to invest significantly in UNIX, which is in decline, and not as much in NT. Consequently, he said at the time, the firm had decided to dominate the NT space as much as it could. In his opinion, it would give Dell a greater share of a faster-growing market. In terms of the Internet, he believes that virtually everybody is going to buy their computer over the 'net in five or ten years. Dell Computer will dominate that market and have a leadership position in sales through it.

◆ *Consider add-on opportunities.* Yes, with all the other growth, Michael Dell keeps his eye out for add-on businesses. This doesn't mean wild diversification or looking at cash on our balance sheet and saying, 'Hey, we've got lots of money, let's go spend it.' Our focus is on clearly connected businesses."

The company had grown so large that Dell couldn't determine how each unit's revenues and costs added up into the whole. Dell Computer needed to refocus on fiscal health and install better management controls. Describing his feelings in 1993, Dell told a reporter, "I felt a gradual panicking. There was a period when every piece of news I heard got worse and worse and worse." He recalled how at one point he and the new chief financial officer were rushing through Heathrow Airport to catch a plane to Ireland. Meredith told Dell that "he saw a silver lining in the notebook disaster – it had revealed that the company's information systems and management had not kept pace with its rapid growth. Dell stopped short. 'Tom,' he said, 'you have a warped sense of humor.' "

Dell has repeatedly talked about how mistakes can become opportunities if one learns from them. And he clearly practices what he preaches. For instance, Dell kept on engineers hired to complete a major product that customers turned thumbs down on, and he encouraged them to focus attention on market needs; in the process, they all discovered that it wasn't always best to develop their own technology. "Two years ago," Dell told Dan McGraw of *US News & World Report,* "we would have told you we were going to do everything. We've learned that doesn't work very well. It's actually much harder to decide what you're not going to do."

Clearly, though, Dell had heard his financial officer. The company had to forsake growth for growth's sake and replace it with a strategy that would let it control the spurts of growth to come. Dell hired a more experienced management team from companies like Motorola, Hewlett-Packard, and Apple. The additions included Mort Topfer, as co-chairman, who had run Motorola's paging business. Topfer was hired to run the day-to-day business operations at Dell. The company was also to refocus its efforts on direct sales, the marketing means it had perfected.

As executives listen to Dell today, it is important that they recognize how important the trials of 1993 were to today's successful Dell Computer. Dell himself has said that they made it easier for him to accept Meredith's recommendation "to change the orientation of the company away from growth, growth,

growth to liquidity, profitability, and growth, which has become a real mantra for the company.'

Given the youth of its founder, however, Dell Computer is carefully watched by investment analysts. For example, in 1997, Dell watchers began to suggest that the company might be in for big problems. Doubts continued about the application of the direct model overseas as Dell expanded operations to China. Michael Dell found himself defending his decisions, which has proven wise. Dell was on its way to becoming a major player in China. Although the competition in China is indeed intense, Dell's choice of the direct model has meant that the firm did not go head-to-head against entrenched local market leaders. And it is working successfully.

WATCH THE COMPETITORS

What about the actions of competitors? The competitors think they are gaining on Dell. In 1997, Hewlett-Packard bragged that its inventories were down 30 percent and reseller inventory would be down to two weeks shortly. "Once we do that," said HP's Jim Mcdonnell, "Dell has got no cost advantage. Zip." Further, HP placed assembly responsibility of many of its PCs on resellers. But investors weren't impressed. They remembered that Dell had virtually no inventory and no reseller markup.

By the same year, IBM already had resellers finish machines, something it embarked on two years before. That helped lower inventories and reduce costs for it, too, but it also increased IBM's reliance on resellers. How about Compaq?

Dell's biggest competitor projected that its effort to streamline the delivery process would enable it to further cut costs. Compaq chief financial officer, Earl Mason, said his firm was the lowest cost provider "period." For 80 percent of its corporate orders, Compaq would customize PCs in its own plants and ship them directly. For smaller and more complex orders – about 20 percent of shipments – it would deliver half-finished PCs to resellers who would handle final assembly and configuration.

None of these firms has yet beaten Dell at its own game.

Yes, analysts keep a watchful eye on the firm. When Dell Computer's stock slipped for two weeks (in February 1999), analysts again questioned the firm's financial position. Market attention focused on a Dell competitor Gateway despite its reputation for poor service. Gateway had developed a three-pronged marketing strategy that many thought would change the future of the PC industry, and enable the once-outcast Gateway to surpass Dell. But by early March of 1999 Dell announced two major developments. First, there was the firm's e-commerce Web site Gigabuys.com from which he would sell 30,000-plus Dell products, including software printers and even games. As Michael Kwatinetz of Credit Suisse First Boston described the move, "Through Gigabuys, Dell can build a stronger, longer-lasting relationship with customers than by simply selling them a box."

What was the second development? Dell signed a $16 billion contract with IBM for components used in the very large computers that it sells to major companies, thereby strengthening Dell's business in that market. Walter Winnitzki of Hambrecht & Quist told the press, "Essentially it's a marriage of one company that has terrific technology to one with great marketing."

As Dell continues its hypergrowth, there is no question that the competition is learning from it and making efforts to emulate it. And the battle is heating up. IBM and Compaq have both become better at managing inventories. In retail outlets, customers of Compaq can go to its Web site and specify their PC with the help of the salesperson beside them. This way, customers get the best of both worlds – the retailer adds value but inventory is kept lean. Compaq head Eckhard Pfeiffer believes that it is possible to offer direct sales but also maintain traditional distribution channels. Not so, says Dell. It will create "channel conflict," perhaps thinking about that early time when his own firm, in its infancy, practiced both direct and retail sales, creating mixed management messages for future planning.

"Executives must pay attention to how their companies create value in both the physical world and the virtual world. Those who understand how to master both can create and extract value in the most efficient and effective manner."
– Jeffrey F. Rayport and John J. Sviokla, "Exploiting the Virtual Value Chain," *Harvard Business Review on Strategies for Growth*

Pfeiffer also has questioned Dell's ability to satisfy customers with wide-area networks and the Internet. Investors wonder, too, whether Dell will enter the $1000 market or market for small Internet-access devices. Compaq is devoting considering time and money on the last. But R&D at Dell is lean and questions exist about whether it is too lean to address such a shift in the industry.

What does Michael Dell say? The Web will drive PC sales and streamline the way Dell sells PCs directly, referring to Dell.com. In his opinion, the PC will play an even more important role in connecting telephone, pager, car, and TV. Internet-connected devices won't cause us to scuttle our PCs; rather, they will make information via the Web more valuable and consequently the PC more important. Firms will change PCs every three years so sales should be steady. High-speed broadband Internet access will cause those not yet on the Internet to dip their toes into the surf. "The market will consume as much bandwidth as the telcos can deliver," Dell told a reporter. According to Dell, more bandwidth will mean more demanding computer and server applications and therefore more new computer sales. At the high end of the market, growth will be in high-speed servers. At the low end, sales momentum will be with limited-functionality devices. And the bulk of the market will be high-speed connectivity.

In Dell's view, broadband access will accelerate information flow, increasing Dell's capacity to add value. Tom Spring, writing up an interview with Michael Dell in *PC World Online*, quoted Dell as saying, "The technology can be a tool that lets Dell become a broker of marketplace information, able to streamline communication between customers and suppliers." Further, in his view, broadband-enhanced multimedia applications represent a "golden opportunity" to send Dell's online pitch to consumers – the equivalent of a 24-hour infomercial. Dell sees a time when his site will host online conferences, broadcast programming on how to get the most out of your Dell PC and, most important, push new system sales.

BIBLIOGRAPHY

Ansley, Robert L., "Managing a Successful Expansion," *Security Management,* October 1993.

"Channel Surfing: Michael Dell of Dell Computer Corporation," *Institutional Investor,* May 1997.

Cohan, Peter S., *e-Profit: High Payoff Strategies for Capturing the E-Commerce Edge*, AMACOM, New York 2000.

Dell, Michael and Fredman, Catherine, *Direct from Dell: Strategies That Revolutionized an Industry*, HarperBusiness, New York 1999.

Harvard Business Review on Strategies for Growth, Harvard Business School Press, Cambridge, MA 1999.

Jacob, Rahul, "The Resurrection of Michael Dell," *Fortune*, September 18, 1995.

Kirkpatrick, David, "Now Everyone in PCs Wants to Be Like Mike," *Fortune*, September 8, 1997.

Kover, Amy, "Never Bet Against Michael Dell," *Fortune,* March 29, 1999.

March, Richard, "Dell Computer Corporation sheds Its One-Man Management Image," *PC Week*, May 1, 1989.

March, Richard, "Dell Slows Its Micro Channel Plans," *PC Week,* August 1, 1988.

McGraw, Dan, "The Kid Bytes Back," *U.S. News & World Report*, December 1, 1994.

Meyer, Peter. *Warp-Speed Growth: Managing the Fast-Track Business Without Sacrificing Time, People, and Money*, AMACOM, New York, 2000.

"Michael Dell's Plan for the Rest of the Decade," *Fortune*, June 9, 1997.

"Personal Computers," *The Economist*, February 20, 1999.

Spring, Tom, "Michael Dell: Superfast Internet Access Will Change E-Commerce," *PC World Online*, April 9, 1999.

Rosch, Winn L., "Falling Prices Signal a Troubled Year for Hard-Disk Vendors," *PC Week*, December **** DAY? **** 1985.

Serwer, Andrew E. "Michael Dell Turns the PC World Inside Out," *Fortune*, September 8, 1997.

Tomasko, Robert M. *Go for Growth: Five Paths to Profit and Success – Choose the Right One for You and Your Company*, John Wiley & Sons, New York 1996.

INDEX